CENTER FOR EDUCATIONAL RESEARCH AND INNOVATION

INDICATORS OF EDUCATION SYSTEMS

DECISION-MAKING IN 14 OECD EDUCATION SYSTEMS

ORGANISATION FOR ECONOMIC CO-OPERATION AND DEVELOPMENT

ORGANISATION FOR ECONOMIC CO-OPERATION AND DEVELOPMENT

Pursuant to Article 1 of the Convention signed in Paris on 14th December 1960, and which came into force on 30th September 1961, the Organisation for Economic Co-operation and Development (OECD) shall promote policies designed:

— to achieve the highest sustainable economic growth and employment and a rising standard of living in Member countries, while maintaining financial stability, and thus to contribute to the development of the world economy;
— to contribute to sound economic expansion in Member as well as non-member countries in the process of economic development; and
— to contribute to the expansion of world trade on a multilateral, non-discriminatory basis in accordance with international obligations.

The original Member countries of the OECD are Austria, Belgium, Canada, Denmark, France, Germany, Greece, Iceland, Ireland, Italy, Luxembourg, the Netherlands, Norway, Portugal, Spain, Sweden, Switzerland, Turkey, the United Kingdom and the United States. The following countries became Members subsequently through accession at the dates indicated hereafter: Japan (28th April 1964), Finland (28th January 1969), Australia (7th June 1971), New Zealand (29th May 1973) and Mexico (18th May 1994). The Commission of the European Communities takes part in the work of the OECD (Article 13 of the OECD Convention).

The Centre for Educational Research and Innovation was created in June 1968 by the Council of the Organisation for Economic Co-operation and Development and all Member countries of the OECD are participants.

The main objectives of the Centre are as follows:

— *to promote and support the development of research activities in education and undertake such research activities where appropriate;*
— *to promote and support pilot experiments with a view to introducing and testing innovations in the educational system;*
— *to promote the development of co-operation between Member countries in the field of educational research and innovation.*

The Centre functions within the Organisation for Economic Co-operation and Development in accordance with the decisions of the Council of the Organisation, under the authority of the Secretary-General. It is supervised by a Governing Board composed of one national expert in its field of competence from each of the countries participating in its programme of work.

Publié en français sous le titre :
LES PROCESSUS DE DÉCISION DANS 14 SYSTÈMES ÉDUCATIFS DE L'OCDE

Foreword

Changes in the patterns of the division of authority in educational decision-making are currently taking place in many countries. Although the overall impression is that restructuring is moving towards devolving authority to lower administrative levels (for instance, the school district, or the school) and away from central administrations, examples of centralisation on certain types of decisions persist. As is apparent from the relevant educational administration literature, the distinction between decentralised and centralised systems is far too crude to do justice to the many-facetted nature of decision-making in education. For instance, in several countries there is an explicit policy to combine devolution of authority concerning teaching processes with more centralised output-control.

International comparisons can be seen as the "royal road" to learning about the merits of the many possible ways of distributing decision-making authority over levels and aspects of education. Stated in research-terminology, decision-making patterns are defined at the national level, which implies that variance can only be studied by making international comparisons or by comparing changes over time within countries.

In the study described in this report, a three-dimensional framework was used to study the levels, the types and modes of decision-making in 14 OECD countries. The results have also been summarized as indicators, published by the OECD in *Education at a Glance* (1992, 1993 and 1995). This report, however, gives more detailed information about the methods used and also provides more detailed results. The international coverage and the differentiated conceptual framework make this study one of a kind and require reading for educational decision-makers and researchers active in educational administration.

The fact that the study is part of the CERI project on international indicators of education systems (INES project) provides the very interesting opportunity to repeat the study during the next couple of years. In this way, the fairly dynamic picture concerning the division of authority in educational decision-making in many countries can be documented. The division of the INES project, from which the study was initiated (Network C which was responsible for measuring indicators of schools and school processes; see *Measuring the Quality of Schools,* OECD, 1995), is presently preparing such a follow-up study. Although Network C was the organisational setting from which the study originated, the work was carried out semi-independently by a French-Swiss team, headed by Denis Meuret from the French Ministry of Education including Jacques Prod'hom and Eugene Stocker of the Swiss Documentation Center on Education.

This report is published on the responsibility of the Secretary-General of the OECD. It represents the views of the authors and does not necessarily reflect those of the OECD or of its Member countries.

As this book was going to press, we learned of the death of Jacques Prod'hom, one of the chief sources of inspiration and authors of this work. He was closely involved in conceiving this volume and was particularly concerned with seeing it published. This volume is dedicated to him.

Jaap Scheerens
Chairman Network C
INES project

Table of Contents

Tables and Figures

Introduction

This study compares the decision-making processes in the education systems of a number of OECD countries, with the term "process" in this case being taken to mean not only the manner in which decisions are taken but also the level at which they are taken.

Indeed, it is debatable whether, 20 years ago, the process of decision-making within an education system would even have been considered as a characteristic worth mentioning. At most, teachers in so-called "decentralised" systems and those in "centralised" systems might have argued about the relative prestige of their profession within one or the other type of system, with the first emphasising the qualities required to discern the kind of knowledge that each child was likely to assimilate, and the second retorting that the republican majesty of the national curriculum was alone capable of reflecting the universal nature of knowledge. For their part, the policy-makers and administrators in charge of these education systems were concerned more with the structure of the system than that of the decision-making process.

In a number of countries, changes have been made in the decision-making process over the last 15 years (see Annex 5). It would seem that the reasons for the reforms that have been introduced are of two kinds:

a) In some cases, the decision-making process has been the subject of debates going well beyond education and concerning the role of the State, devolution or the decentralisation of government activity, and the role of competition within the public service. Directly or indirectly, these debates stem from a concern for the effectiveness and equality of the education system. Their frame of reference is technical rather than policy-oriented, even though they may call upon ideological principles and lead to institutional changes that have a substantial impact from a policy standpoint;

b) In other cases, the upsurge in regional sentiment has sometimes resulted in the assigning of virtually all powers to subnational entities. In Belgium, for example, the "linguistic communities" manage their education systems independently. Spain's "autonomous communities" have virtually complete responsibility for their education systems. For the academic year 1990/91 they were responsible for roughly half Spain's schoolchildren. In this case, the willingness to transfer authority with regard to education stems from the recognition of this as one of the attributes of sovereignty and a symbol of cultural identity. The

9

frame of reference for the debate, in this case, is more policy-related than technical.

In fact, there are very few developed countries which, like Germany and Switzerland, have not during the past 20 years reformed in some way or other the division of authority within their education system. In the United States, the powers of the individual states – and many schools – have been increased at the expense of the school districts.

In the Nordic countries, a radical reform of the mid-1980s transferred most of the central government's powers to the municipalities. The national level no longer intervenes, via the parliament and the government, except to determine the overall framework for education, and through a "National Education Agency". The national authorities, however, retain their powers as regards statistics, evaluation and the development of the system.

France has, in a highly visible manner, devolved a number of powers to the elected regional assemblies and, in a somewhat less visible manner, even more powers to the regional tiers of central government and to schools. Currently, for example, French secondary schools are free to choose, within the framework of an overall allocation of hours and more flexible national curricula, whether they wish to have a teacher for a particular subject.

There are also a number of instances where powers at the national level have been increased at the expense of the local level. In England, for example, the powers of the LEAs (Local Education Authorities) have been eroded by the 1988 Act to the benefit of the schools and, on the other hand, by the introduction of a national curriculum for the greater part of the timetable. New Zealand has taken this approach to its extreme: since 1989, the government has been applying a programme known as "tomorrow's schools", whereby all of the powers are concentrated at two levels only, *i.e.* the school and the national level.

In short, it would seem that, in most cases, powers have been transferred in one of three directions: from the national to the regional level (Belgium, Spain), from the intermediate levels (local in particular) to the levels at either extreme (*e.g.* England, New Zealand, the United States), or from the national to the local level (Nordic countries).

Apparently, therefore, the policymakers responsible for education systems nowadays consider the division of powers, and more broadly the decision-making process, as one of the most powerful "levers" in their possession.

It is very likely that the decision-making process has a direct effect on the quality of the decisions taken (their relevance with regard to objectives, their suitability in the light of circumstances), on the manner in which they are accepted and applied by those they concern, on the nature of the pressure groups that can influence them, on the duration of the process of preparing these decisions and on the variety of situations they give rise to. In addition, this process illustrates, at least in the case of the public systems of education, the nature of the relationships between the central authorities, the schools and the users: it will involve to a greater or lesser degree those concerned by these decisions, and it will be public and transparent to a greater or lesser degree.

10

These characteristics in their turn have a definite influence on the effectiveness of the education and on its equality. This influence may, however, not be linear: a given decision-making process may improve effectiveness as regards basic learning but have less positive results in terms of emphasising, encouraging and giving impetus to cultural activities. It may promote equality in general, through a greater concern for the disparities between pupils, but at the same time prove to be ineffective in dealing with the inequality between two particular groups. A particular decision-making process may also assign greater influence either to actors concerned primarily with effectiveness over the short term, or to actors more worried about the long term.

There are therefore several dimensions which a decision-making process may affect. It has to be said that policymakers have had to construct their reforms without the help of any empirical knowledge whatsoever as to the nature and likely outcome of such action.

This study is not designed to provide such knowledge, but only to make it possible to gather this by providing a tentative formalised description of decision-making processes in a number of countries. It is solely by attempting in this way to characterise decision-making processes that they can be related not only to effectiveness and equality, but also to the cost of education in each country.

This study is an outcome of the CERI project on international indicators of education systems. It will also have therein (in part) its culmination, since it is to be hoped that the other indicators developed during the course of this project, coupled with those describing the decision-making processes, will shed some light on the question of the effects of these processes.

This study also attempts to provide not only the authorities but also the public with a greater insight into the decision-making structure of their education system, insofar as a comparison, a reference from one system to another, improves the perception and understanding one has of the system. In this respect, the study also bears witness to the concern for transparency shown by the authorities who agreed to reply to the questionnaire on which it is based and to allow the findings to be exploited.

Wherever there is a debate on the decision-making processes, it is often heated: in France, for example, where certain political persuasions would like to increase the powers of the regional authorities; and in Austria, where the two main political parties disagreed about whether the national level should authorise the schools themselves or only the regional level to make changes in the curriculum. References to other countries are often made in this debate but, given the present state of knowledge in this respect, this tends to be confined to a number of broad conceptions, to one or two outstanding features of each system (the dual system in Germany, pre-school provision in France, the single school up to age 14 in Denmark, etc.) or to certain major trends in recent years (*e.g.* the increasing autonomy of schools). In either case, the information used, being fragmentary, can be misleading.

For the future, the aim is to define more clearly the considerations involved in choosing a decision-making process; for the moment, the aim is to enlighten the authorities and the public, and provide food for thought in the various countries: these are the reasons that have prompted this attempt to come up with a formalised and systematic description of the decision-making processes in those OECD countries that agreed to take part in this exercise.

Such a venture is not without its risks. It might be thought that a decision-making process defies any attempt at comprehensive analysis. The actual detailed functioning of an education system depends on an infinite number of decisions taken every moment by an infinite number of actors (pupils, parents, teachers, administrators, etc.). What is more, each decision can be depicted by a vast number of variables, since it can be considered from a number of different angles.

Even when this is confined, as here, to the *decisions that form the framework* within which the actors can operate, a number of problems arise. How does one "add together" decisions, the list of which might seem arbitrary and whose respective importance it is impossible to compare, and decisions that may be taken in a different manner whenever different subsystems are being considered, and where these subsystems may be either geographical or institutional? How does one compare education systems of a very different size, where there may be as many pupils in a local area as there are in the whole of another country?

New Zealand, for example, has stripped the intermediate levels of virtually every function within the education system, dividing all of the powers between the national level and the schools. How can a situation such as this be meaningfully compared with that in the United States or even Spain?

For two reasons it was decided that a genuine attempt at measurement should be made in order to determine whether these obstacles could be overcome. One was that, however imperfect the representation that would be thus obtained, it would be less inaccurate than those that exist at present. The second was that, by endeavouring to construct an initial description, it would be possible to identify specific difficulties that one could subsequently attempt to overcome during the second stage of the operation.

The data analysed hereunder are the result of an interrogation (the third of its kind), the aim of each of these interrogations being to resolve the problems raised by the previous one.

Without any doubt, these interrogations can be improved and, accordingly, this work must be considered as marking a stage where an attempt has been made to establish an accurate list of unresolved difficulties and remaining ambiguities.

In addition, it should be said that describing the decision-making processes proved to be less difficult than had been imagined at the outset. The vast number and variety of arguments that are put forward in the pedagogical or policy discussions on the advantages of one or other process conceals to some extent the fact that, for the most part, the decisions in question are relatively few in number and can be described with the help of a fairly small set of variables.

What is more, the difficult question of the respective importance of each decision proved not to be insurmountable. Contrary even to the expectations of the authors themselves, tests carried out using various different systems of weighting yielded relatively similar results, as will be seen hereafter.

Lastly, other problems were resolved through the use, at a number of stages, of two methodological "tools":

a) Agreement between experts. A proposition was considered as valid if two experts, or two groups of experts, after examining it independently, agreed that this was so;

b) The threshold concept. This served to focus the analysis on the main features of each system by excluding those situations which concern too small a proportion of pupils.

This study describes the decision-making process in the education systems of 14 OECD countries in 1990/91 – based on the structure of these systems as defined in national legislation and regulations at that time – for both public and private education, and for three stages: primary, lower-secondary and upper-secondary education. Nursery schools, special education and higher education were not included.

A total of 34 types of decision were taken as the basis for analysing the decision-making process in four fields of operation within the education system: the organisation of instruction, the planning of education and the establishment of the structures within which it is delivered, personnel management, resource allocation and use.

The decisions themselves are classified in accordance with the field to which they apply, the institutional level at which they are taken and the way in which they are taken. For the purposes of this analysis, four levels and three modes of decision-making were specified.

The 14 countries covered by the study are as follows: Austria, Belgium, Denmark, Finland, France, Germany, Ireland, New Zealand, Norway, Portugal, Spain, Sweden, Switzerland and the United States.

Finally, it should be mentioned that since 1990/91, when this study was carried out, the decision-making processes in a number of countries have changed.

For example, in Finland the National Board of Education has lost its remaining administrative powers, thus diminishing the importance of the national level in the decision-making process; in the United States, more schools have become autonomous and manage their own affairs, etc. The reader must therefore bear in mind that this study, like any other analysis of this kind, is valid only for a particular period in time.

This study is in two parts: the first describes the way in which it was carried out and the problems still to be overcome; the second sets out the results that were obtained. The accompanying annexes contain a set of raw data together with the questionnaires and forms used to collect the information.

Part I
The Procedure Adopted

This part describes the methodology adopted and its implementation. This is intended both to enable the reader to compare the results obtained, as set out in Part II, with the way in which they were arrived at, and to take a stage further the thinking and discussions regarding methodology on the basis of the difficulties encountered and the solutions that, in some cases, have been found.

Methodology

This study had neither earlier research nor existing data on which it could draw. What this meant therefore was that a concept had to be defined and, on the basis of this, a questionnaire designed to obtain the necessary information in the various countries concerned.

The approach adopted focused mainly on the legal, regulatory and administrative aspects governing education. In other words, the decision-making process described herein is, for obvious practical reasons, that defined in the relevant legislation and regulations and not the "real" process insofar as this may be different.

The actual investigation of the decision-making process as defined above meant establishing first a list of relevant decisions, second the levels and modes of decision-making to be considered, third the scope of the study and lastly a technique for aggregating the results. These four aspects are dealt with in turn hereunder.

Selecting the decisions

The questionnaires (see Annex 4) contained 35 questions covering the main decisions *affecting the operation of an education system and which in addition can be taken at the school level.*

The initial object of the study was to ascertain the school's degree of autonomy within the education system. This was subsequently broadened because it was very soon realised that the school's autonomy depended also on the distance that separated it from the other bodies that decided on its behalf. Nonetheless, it was agreed to retain the original idea of looking only at decisions that could conceivably be taken by the school itself within a completely decentralised system. Consequently, the study did not cover some of the more important types of decision (the duration of compulsory education, arrangements for providing financial assistance to pupils, comprehensive rather than streamed education, the training to be given to teachers or school heads, etc.).

The list of decisions was drawn up by the Franco-Swiss Working Group in charge of the study and submitted to members of Network C (on the measurement of the quality of schools) of the OECD/CERI international indicators of education systems project.[1] It was amended after an initial test carried out during the second half of 1990 in seven countries that had volunteered their services. The definition of some of these decisions was clarified for the countries concerned during the course of the verification procedure in early 1993.

The decisions studied were classified into four fields:
– Organisation of instruction.
– Planning of education and creation of the structures in which it is delivered.
– Personnel management.
– Resource allocation and use.

These categories make for more targeted analyses and the construction of specific indicators.

The decisions (items) selected were as follows:

a) *Organisation of Instruction*
P1   Bodies determining the school attended;
P2   Decisions affecting school careers;
P3   Length of schooling time;
P4   Selection of school books;
P5   Methods of grouping pupils;
P6   The organisation of aid for school work;
P7   Teaching methods;
P8   Methods of evaluating pupils' normal work.

b) *Planning and Structures*
S1   Creation and closure of schools;
S2   Creation and suppression of classes;
S3   Planning of courses on the basis of subject matters;
S4-1 Choice of range of subject matters;
S4-2 Choice of range of courses;
S5   Course content;
S6   Structure and content of qualifying examinations;
S7   Credentialling.

c) *Personnel Management*
R1   Hiring or dismissal of staff:
R1-1 School principal;
R1-2 Teachers;
R1-3 Others.

R2   Duties and conditions of service:
R2-1   School principal;
R2-2   Teachers;
R2-3   Others.
R3   Setting salary levels:
R3-1   School principal;
R3-2   Teachers;
R3-3   Others.
R4   Influence on staff careers:
R4-1   School principal;
R4-2   Teachers;
R4-3   Others.

d) Resources
F1   Allocation of resources for:
F1-1   Teaching staff;
F1-2   Other staff;
F1-3   Capital expenditure;
F1-4   Operating expenditure.
F2   Utilisation of resources by the school:
F2-1   Staff;
F2-2   Capital expenditure;
F2-3   Operating expenditure.

The contours, so to speak, of each decision (item) are in some cases self-evident, *e.g.* for P1 (Who determines the school attended?). However, this is not always the case: for example, decisions affecting careers or conditions of service (R4, R2) are multidimensional. A teacher's conditions of service, for instance, depend on the convenience of his hours, his pupils' attitude to school, their level and the size of his classes. Decisions such as these have been classified together under a single item whenever it seemed probable that they are taken by the same authority and interrelated.

Thus, whenever a school principal decides on a teacher's timetable, he decides at one and the same time the different parameters of the teacher's conditions of service. By contrast, the question of the subject matters taught in a school (S3, S4–1, S4–2, S5) has been treated as four separate decisions, because it was considered that the decision-makers for each of these four aspects of the question could be different, at least in some countries. Since this proved to be the case (see Annex 3.3), this separation was maintained.

The groupings used here might well, of course, be criticised. For example, Norway pointed out that it was not a good idea to have combined duties with conditions of service under the same item (R2) because these two types of decision, although they both had a bearing on the pleasantness or unpleasantness of the work, were often taken at a different level.[2]

The significance of a question depends on its interrelationship with the others. For example, a teacher's salary depends, among other things, on the stage he has reached in his career (R4), the number of extra hours he may work or the special allowances he may receive to compensate for the difficulty of his conditions of service (R2). The decision R3 (setting salary levels) needs therefore to be treated as if all other things were equal, notably with regard to conditions of service and career stage, given that the decisions with regard to these are dealt with in R2 and R4.

Should the major educational decisions be taken into account, despite the fact that they are taken in the same way in all countries? For example, at ISCED stage 2, all of the countries stated that the methods of evaluating pupils' normal work (P8) were decided at the school level, in some cases within a framework set by a higher authority. This is, however, the only item where this situation applies. Nonetheless, it was felt that it should not be left out of the analysis of decision-making levels.

This is a moot point. In support of this position, it can be argued that the only criterion for retaining or omitting a decision should be its effect on the education received by pupils. If the decisions considered are only those where countries diverge, their differences will be over-exaggerated. On the other hand, it can be argued that if, throughout all of the existing (or possible?) education systems, the same solution is adopted, there is no point in taking it into account, just as there is no point in adopting as a criterion of physical resemblance between two individuals the fact that they each have a head.

The adoption of the first of these two alternatives demonstrates that a functionalist approach was preferred to a relativist approach. The nature of an education system is determined by all of the characteristics that enable it to fulfil its function (*i.e.* the education delivered to pupils) and not by the characteristics that differentiate it from other systems.

The 35 decisions were classified into four fields, two concerning the way educational activity is organised (the organisation of instruction, planning and structures) and two the inputs that this activity requires (personnel, resources). These last two would obviously figure in the analysis of any system.

Classifying these 35 decisions into groups means that we are able to adopt an approach by broad category, similar to the usual method for comparing education systems, starting out from a more detailed approach. For example, in the case of the hiring of a teacher, a distinction is made between the decision to allocate the necessary resources (F1-1, F1-2), the decision to use these resources for a particular post (a maths teacher, English teacher or a nurse) (F2-1) and, lastly, the decision to recruit a particular person for this post (R1). Although all these decisions are frequently taken by the same authority and even at one and the same time, they need to be kept separate so that the analysis is able to handle the most widely differing decision-making structures. This, in fact, makes for a more sophisticated approach to decision-making than those commonly used. It is also more detailed than the approach adopted by the Eurydice European Unit for studying the distribution of powers in the area of education in 12 European Union member states, *i.e.* general legislation, definition of streams, definition of curricula, certification, funding (Eurydice European Unit, 1991).

Levels and modes of decision-making

Four levels or loci of decision-making are specified:

- The school: this covers decisions taken internally, including those that teachers are free to take on their own initiative.
- The Lower Intermediate level (LI) is the locus of decision-making close to the school. In most cases it is the municipal authority, occasionally the district authority.
- The Upper Intermediate level (UI) is the level immediately below that of central government. It may be an elected regional authority, some for the specific purpose of looking after education, or a decentralised service of central government. A system of indices was devised so as to identify these, but this was rarely used by respondents.
- Central government: this is the decision-making level furthest removed from the school from an institutional standpoint. It is the entity that is represented at the OECD.

It goes without saying that terms "lower" and "upper" as used here do not carry any connotation of inferiority or inequality between these levels, but simply denote a topographical classification of the various components of a political-administrative structure in the form of a pyramid where the elements that are fewer in number are "above" those that are more numerous.

Three aspects of these definitions need to be noted:

- "The school" does not necessarily mean "the school principal". It may mean the teachers as a body, each teacher individually or a board of governors. A board of governors must be responsible for one, and only one, school. A municipal authority, even though it may be in charge of only one school, since it deals with other things than its school, forms part of the lower intermediate level (LI). A school board in Quebec or a primary school district in France also belong to level LI despite the fact that they are sometimes responsible for only a few schools.
- Given that UI was defined as the level closer to central government and LI as that closer to the school, some difficulties arose as to how to position any other intermediate levels that might exist. Countries were allowed to add extra levels on the questionnaire formats, in which case these additional columns, for calculation purposes, were incorporated in LI. This was the case in Belgium where, for ISCED 2 and 3, LI includes local boards, the municipal and provincial authorities, and the "community autonomous education boards" (ARGO).
  Sometimes the countries themselves assigned these additional levels to LI or UI. In this case, they sometimes took a different approach. Portugal, for example, integrated within LI (for ISCED 1) an intermediate level between the municipalities (LI) and the regional departments of education (UI) because "decisions taken at this level tend to be transferred to the municipalities". France combined the department with the region (UI), confining LI solely to the municipal authorities. However, this type of problem arose only in these three countries and Austria.

- Although the term "central government", for the purposes of this study, was taken to mean the entities represented at the OECD, a number of countries have education systems that are so distinct that it was even considered at one time that the highest level of aggregation should be the education system rather than central government: for example, the system of Belgium's French-speaking community rather than Belgium as a whole. Applying this principle, however, would have meant adding unduly to the number of units studied: it would have meant, for example, taking 26 education systems for Switzerland alone, and perhaps 50 for the United States. The approach that was adopted (*i.e.* working on the basis of Member countries rather than education systems) means that the analysis reflects any devolution of powers to a "regional" level, rather than this level being simply placed at the head. It makes it easier to compare indicators derived from this analysis of decision-making processes with other international education indicators, as well as with other economic and social data (*e.g.* youth unemployment rates, GDP growth rates, etc.) which, in their case, are more often than not for the country as a whole. Clearly, however, in order to study the consequences of these decision-making processes, the ideal would be to focus on entities where the processes are identical – countries or groups of countries, or systems within a country – and to (re)calculate economic and social indicators for these same entities. This would in all probability be a rather complex operation.

Of the four levels defined (the school, lower intermediate, upper intermediate, central government) some additional explanation is needed regarding the two intermediate levels since their component elements can differ quite substantially from one country to another. These two intermediate levels in each country are identified in Table 1. When making certain international comparisons, this information needs to be borne in mind.

It should also be said that the instructions given to respondents did not specify whether the structure of levels within a country could be altered for the different ISCED stages. In fact, respondents took the view that this structure should not be altered. Consequently, in the case of France, the commune and the education district (*circonscription pédagogique*) make up Level LI because they have responsibilities with regard to primary schools. They have none as regards as secondary schools but nevertheless continue to figure as Level LI, with the result that, in France, the level closest to the secondary school is not LI but UI.

Modes of decision-making are classified into three categories:
- Full autonomy, subject only to any constraints contained in the constitution or in legislation outside the education system itself (*e.g.* legislation regarding a guaranteed minimum wage). Respondents were asked to use the letter "A" to denote decisions taken in this manner.
- In conjunction or after consultation with bodies located at another level within the education system. In this case, before taking a particular decision, the level which decides is required to consult the body to which it will apply. It is not required to accept the opinion expressed by this body, but it is required seek it.
It should be noted that, in this study, a decision is not considered as being taken in consultation unless the regulations stipulate that it involves two different levels

Table 1. **Designation of the levels in 14 countries in the local language**

	Level LI	Level UI	Country
Austria	Bezirk	Bundesland	Österreich
Belgium	Autonome raad van gemeenshap ordering (ARGO). Pouvoirs organisateurs communaux et provinciaux	Ministry of each linguistic community	Belgique
Denmark	Kommune	Amt	Denmark
Finland	Kunta	Lääni	Suomi
France	Circonscription or Commune	Département or Académie or Région	République française
Germany	Gemeinde/Bezirk	Land	Deutschland
Ireland	*	*	Eire
New Zealand	*	*	New Zealand
Norway	Skolestyret	Fylkesskole styret	Norge
Portugal	Autarquia	Dir. Region. de Educaçao	Portugal
Spain	Provincia	Comunidad autonoma	España
Sweden	Kommun	*	Sverige
Switzerland	Commune	Canton	Confédération helvétique
United States	District	State	United States

* This level does not exist.
  This table does not cover private education.

within the system, *e.g.* that the lower intermediate level (LI) has to seek the opinion of school X on the candidature of M. as a biology teacher before recruiting him and assigning him to school X. In this case, the replies had to show a "B" in the column for the decision-making level and a "b" in the column for the level consulted.

If the decision is taken in conjunction by two bodies at the same level – for example, if the regional administration decides after a meeting at which the regional teachers' unions were able to express their point of view on the proposed decision – this decision is considered in this study as having been taken at this level (UI) in full autonomy and not in consultation, and an "A" and not a "B" had to be entered in column UI of the reply.

– Independently but within a framework set by a higher authority (*e.g.* a binding law, a pre-established list of possibilities, a budgetary limit, etc.). The replies differentiated between the level at which the decision is taken ("C") and that where the framework is set ("c").

Two examples will help to clarify what is meant by a decision taken within a set framework.

- In ISCED 1 Public, New Zealand stated that the school decides on the length of schooling time (P3) within a framework set at central government level because, as is pointed out in their reply to the questionnaire, central government determines every year the minimum number of days during which schools should be open and the period within which the daily number of hours should be situated.
- In ISCED 2 Public, colleges in France can decide, within the framework of a given budget of teacher-hours set by the rectorate (UI), for what subject matter they would prefer to have an additional teacher. Accordingly, France's reply to the questionnaire states that colleges can decide on the use of their resources in terms of personnel (F2-1) within a framework set by the rectorate.

However, as will be seen later in the section describing the implementation of this methodology, a number of problems of interpretation arose with regard to the use of this decision-making mode.

Scope

The study covers public and private education at ISCED levels 1, 2 and 3. Special, pre-compulsory and higher education are not included.

In the analysis that follows the resulting six subsets will be treated separately. It was felt that to analyse the three stages of education together would have meant, when defining the decision-making process, assigning undue weight to those stages in which more pupils are enrolled.

The emphasis will be placed on ISCED 2 to the extent that the results for the other stages will be presented solely in comparison with ISCED 2, which will be analysed first of all. ISCED 2 was chosen because it is the one that is generally considered to pose many problems, because it accounts for a very large number of pupils and because it has an intermediate position between primary and upper secondary education.

Moreover, it was suggested that the questionnaires for private education should not be filled in unless it accounted for at least 5 per cent of enrolment at the ISCED stage in question, which was the case in only six countries: Belgium, France, Portugal, Spain, United States and Austria for ISCED levels 2 and 3.

In each country, the distinction between public and private education is a clear one, but it is however difficult to provide an all-embracing definition. The difference can be the source of funding (public versus private), the denominational character (usually catholic), public service requirements (to accept everyone without distinction) or compliance with the rules and regulations governing public education. A recent OECD report (OECD, 1994) lists three key variables in characterising public support for private education in each country: the method of financial support, the level of financial support and the degree of independence. What is more, several forms of private education can exist alongside one another within the same country. This creates particular difficulties when studying decision-making processes because these differ – but perhaps less than one would have imagined – depending on the nature of the funding. Without going into detail, a distinction can be drawn between countries where private education has neither subsidies nor constraints – the United States being the best example – and countries where there are two types of private education: the smaller of the two, usually non-denominational, non-subsidised and without constraints, and the other, the larger of the two, usually catholic, heavily subsidised and subject to constraints regarding teachers' qualifications, the curriculum and programmes of study – Portugal and France being good examples of this. It should be added that, in some countries, private education is subsidised, irrespective of whether it is denominational or not – as in Switzerland for instance.

Notwithstanding, what is called private education in this study is what each country describes as such. Table 2 sets out the broad characteristics of private education for the six countries in which it accounts for more than 5 per cent of total enrolment.

Some countries have rather unusual situations: in Ireland, for example, what is termed private education accounts for 2 per cent of primary enrolment and nothing at the secondary level, but 76 per cent of the schools providing public secondary education belonged to catholic institutions and are very akin to what is elsewhere called private education under contract. Furthermore, as we shall be seeing later, Ireland's schools enjoy an autonomy similar to that of private schools in other countries.

In Finland, private education is subsidised. It is subject to the same constraints as public education with regard to teachers' qualifications and the curriculum. These constraints, however, do not apply to Rudolf Steiner schools, which have entered into a special contract with the National Education Council. In Finland, private education accounts for less than 5 per cent of enrolment, except in the case of vocational education

Table 2. **Private education in six OECD countries**

		Percentage of pupils			Heavily subsidised	Constraints
		ISCED 1	ISCED 2	ISCED 3		
Austria	Under contract (*Offentlichkeitsrecht*)	4	7	10	YES	YES
Belgium	Subsidised	42	66	66	YES	YES
France	Under contract	14	20	21	YES	YES
	Non-contractual	1	1	1	NO	NO
Portugal	Under contract	4	6	5	YES	YES
	Non-contractual	1	2	1	NO	NO
Spain	Under contract	31	31	10	YES	YES
	Non-contractual	4	4	17	NO	YES
United States		12	10	8	NO	NO

at ISCED 3. This vocational education has its own specific decision-making process, whereas the process is identical for both the public and private sectors. Accordingly, separate data for the private sector has not been included in this study.

Sweden and Norway have a form of private education (85 per cent subsidised out of public funds), while Switzerland has two (one subsidised, the other not). In these three countries, and for each of the three stages of education, the private sector never accounts for more than 5 per cent of total enrolment.

Aggregation of the replies

The data gathered by means of the questionnaires are a very rich source of information per se but do not make for easy comparative analysis. The task of converting this qualitative information into a quantifiable form constituted therefore one of the major phases of the study. It was a question of expressing in percentage terms the degree of involvement in the decision-making processes according to the level, mode and field of decision-making, and the ISCED level. A detailed explanation of the method of calculation is given below.

On the basis of the data contained in the answers to the questionnaires, a six-dimensional matrix was constructed:

Matrix: $Y (i, j, k, l, m, n)$ where

i = country (14 OECD countries in total)

j = status (public, private)

k = ISCED level (ISCED 1, ISCED 2, ISCED 3)

l = field

$l = 1$: organisation of instruction
$l = 2$: structures
$l = 3$: personnel management
$l = 4$: resources

m = level of decision-making

$m = 1$: school
$m = 2$: lower intermediate level
$m = 3$: upper intermediate level
$m = 4$: central government

n = mode of decision-making

$n = 1$: autonomy
$n = 2$: consultation
$n = 3$: within a set framework

In this way, information for the four fields was compiled. Each comprises a variable number of items (see preceding pages). A field is the reflection of the items that make it up, irrespective of how many there are and the possible absence of any reply to a particular item.

By adding these fields together we obtain the aggregate results for each country by level and mode of decison-making.

By aggregating the data still further we can obtain even broader results such as, for example, decision-making by level, irrespective of field and mode.

Thus, by means of a series of aggregations we can obtain the elements needed for calculating the indicators. Using this matrix it is also possible to construct as many indicators as there are ways of cross-tabulating the variables, from the least to the most aggregated form of data.

In order to make comparisons between countries, the different elements of the matrix are calculated in the form of percentages.

For example, take the case of Sweden as regards public primary education: let us assume that we want to calculate the indicator for decision-making by the school, irrespective of field and mode.

The number of decisions taken, irrespective of mode, is as follows:

Field	School	Intermediate levels (LI + UI)	Central government
Organisation of instruction	7/8	1/8	
Structures	3/8	3/8	2/8
Personnel management	4/12	8/12	
Resources	2/7	5/7	

Thus, the number of decisions taken by the school, irrespective of mode and field is:
$(7/8 + 3/8 + 4/12 + 2/7)/4 = 0.467$, or 47 per cent.

In the case of Sweden, therefore, it can be said that, with respect to public primary education, 47 per cent of the decisions are taken by the school. However, in view of the fact that, for the final processing of the data, the number of usable items in the field "Structures" was seven rather than eight, the figure given for Sweden in Table 9 (Part II) is $(7/8 + 3/7 + 4/12 + 2/7)/4 = 0.48$, *i.e.* 48 per cent and not 47 per cent.

In order to calculate the overall situation, that is to say for the 14 countries as a whole, this is not done by averaging the ratios per country. What is done is to consider that all of the countries have replied to a single questionnaire, as though they were only one country. For example, in order to calculate the importance of the school for the 14 countries as a whole, the ratio of the number of mentions in the column "school" to the total number of mentions is worked out for the 14 countries in total. The difference between this and averaging the ratios is that those countries which did not reply in the case of all of the decisions have somewhat less influence than the others on the overall result. With this method, all of the countries are of identical importance in determining the total, whatever their size.

When an item is not meaningful for a particular situation, it is withdrawn from the list of items making up the field. For example, in many countries the two questions relating to examinations (S6 and S7) were not relevant for ISCED 1 which culminates without an examination of any kind. In this case, the weight of each of the six other items in the field "Planning and Structures" becomes 1/6 instead of 1/8. This stems from the approach adopted, whereby each decision is so to speak a descriptor of the field to which it belongs, the question being to determine how the different levels or modes of decision "share" this field. By the same token, the phrase that will subsequently be used for the sake of convenience, *i.e.* "X per cent of decisions are taken at a given level, or in a given way", is, strictly speaking, incorrect. The correct phrase, albeit somewhat clumsy to use, would be "The weight of a given level, of a given mode, in the decision-making structure is X per cent on the basis of a system of calculation whereby 25 per cent is allocated to each of the four fields, with this 25 per cent being equally divided between each of the items making up the field".

The weight of a single decision (or item) within the magnitudes that will be used in this study depends therefore on the field to which it belongs, *i.e.* 25/8 or 3.12 per cent for an item in "Organisation of Instruction" or in "Planning and Structures", 25/7 or 3.57 per cent for an item in "Resources" and 25/12 or 2.08 per cent for an item in "Personnel Management", wherever replies have been obtained for all of these items. In other words, if one more of the 35 decisions in the study is taken by the school, this will increase the importance of the school as a level in the decision-making process between 2.08 and 3.57 percentage points depending on the field to which decision applies.

In some cases, more than one reply was given for the same decision, within the same country and for the same ISCED level. For example, college teachers (ISCED 2) in France are divided into two *corps* one of which is recruited (R1) at the academy level (UI) and the other at national level; some US schools choose their own school books (P4) within a framework set by the district and the state, whereas others have their textbooks imposed on them by the district (LI); in Finland, the decision-making system for ISCED level 3 is not the same for general and vocational education; lastly, in Spain the system of decision-making for the same ISCED level differs depending on whether this is within a Comunidad autonoma (UI) to which responsibility for education has been devolved.

Two things can occur in a case like these. If the respondent has indicated the number of pupils concerned in each situation, then the weight of the item as just defined (2.08, 3.57, etc.) is divided between the two in proportion to the number of pupils. If the respondent has simply indicated that one situation is the more common of the two, then this will be allocated 66 per cent of the item's weight and the other 33 per cent.

The various decisions taken by schools, the national level or the intermediate levels do not all have the same importance as regards the operation of education systems. Accordingly, some form of *weighting* is needed for items and fields.

However, the system of weighting used in this study is, so to speak, an absence of weighting. Each field has been allocated the same weight, regardless of the number of items per field and the proportion of items for which a reply was received. Items in the same field are not weighted relative to one another.

There are two reasons for what unquestionably places a limitation on this study and what is a problem that will need to be resolved subsequently. A weighting system is necessary if it obviously makes for a more accurate approach. On the one hand, however, devising a scale of weightings would be difficult and, on the other, a series of simulations showed that weighting the decisions did not alter the results as much as one might have imagined.

The system of weighting would need to be the same for all countries and thus be the outcome of a process of consultation.

It would not be impossible to carry out such consultation, but it would come up against a number of problems.

- In reality, the importance of a decision can vary from one country to another. The recruitment of a school principal (R1-1), for example, is a prerogative whose importance differs depending on the legal autonomy of the school and the real power that the head exercises over his school. Likewise, the defining of the content of an examination (S6) is a prerogative whose importance can vary depending on how selective this examination is or how necessary it is for pursuing studies or securing employment.
- A weighting implies a point of view. The weight assigned to a decision can vary depending on whether what is being considered is an education system's effectiveness, its egalitarianism or its participative character. The point of view adopted will naturally depend on each person's preferences but also, objectively, on the scale of the consequences of the decision-making process. Let us suppose that changes in the decision-making process have no influence whatsoever on the effectiveness of the education system but a great deal on its egalitarian character. The decisions would then need to be weighted more in accordance with their influence on its egalitarianism. Conversely, if the weighting is based from the outset on the criterion of egalitarianism, this will increase the chances of finding that it is indeed on this aspect that differences between decision-making processes impinge.
  In fact, the adoption of a system of weighting implies agreement, implicit or explicit, between the countries on the respective importance of these points of view and an iterative process analysing the effects of the decision-making processes. Despite the fact that the absence of a system of weighting is somewhat arbitrary, it is not completely illogical to take this as the starting point for this iterative process.
- The reasons why a country may consider a decision "important" may have nothing to do with its real importance. A decision which may have recently been the subject of controversy will find its importance magnified. Conversely, a decision over which there has been no disagreement will find its importance diminished.

Moreover, it would not be completely meaningless to provide Member countries with a picture which is coloured in this way by a kind of "collective subjectivity", but then this would be another type of decision-making aid, another type of information than that for which every effort would be made to insure that it is based on the objective importance of the various decisions via an estimation of their effects on a series of criteria. A choice has to be made between these two approaches.

27

Simulations were carried out of several systems of weighting. In particular, the respective importance of the four levels (school, LI, UI, central government) within the structure of decision-making for public education at ISCED 2 was calculated using six systems of weighting, the principles of which, described below, were worked out by the Franco-Swiss team in charge of the study:

- Equal weighting of fields and, within each field, equal weighting of items. This is the system of weighting that was used and the one which has been described above.
- The field "Resources" was given a weighting of one and each of the others a weighting of two. Within each field, each item was given a weighting of from one to two in accordance with its "importance". In order to decide on these coefficients, each of the five members of the team compiled a weighting and any differences were discussed until a consensus was reached.
- The weighting, by a coefficient of from one to four, of each decision in accordance with its proximity in relation to the teaching act itself, *i.e.* in accordance with how directly it is linked to the actual situation of a pupil. This system of weighting was calculated by a member of the team and then submitted to the others for approval.
- The weighting, by a coefficient of from one to four, of each decision in accordance with its proximity to the factors determining the effectiveness of classes and schools as defined by means of empirical research on school effectiveness. These factors were taken from the model devised by J. Scheerens as part of a comprehensive analysis of such research on behalf of the international indicators of education systems project (Scheerens, 1992, p.14). In this system of weighting, for example, the decisions regarding the recruitment and management of teaching staff (R1-2, R2-2, R3-2) were considered to be more important than others because many of the factors determining the effectiveness of education depend directly, in the model used, on the behaviour of teachers [high expectations regarding pupils' attainment, ability to interact with the class (support, etc.)]. It should, moreover, be noted that the use of this criterion could lead to importance being assigned to decisions that are outside the scope of this study such as, for example, those affecting the way teacher training is organised. This system of weighting was worked out by a member of the team.
- The weighting of decisions in accordance with their proximity to the teaching act, but retaining an equal weighting for the fields. This is, to some extent, weighting system 3 incorporated within 1.
- Equal weighting of all items.

Some of these systems of weighting introduce, as it were, the absence of any weighting by assigning equal weight either to the different fields or to all 34 decisions.

All of the others are based on the idea that the importance of a decision is proportional to its likely influence on the effectiveness of education. This influence was estimated on the basis of a number of criteria: the intuitive judgment of members of the team, proximity to the education process and proximity to the variables related to the effectiveness of schools. The general principle, therefore, is that the less a decision is likely to change the effectiveness of pupils' education, the less it matters, in order to characterise a country's decision-making structure, at what level it is taken.

General principles of another kind could give rise to other systems of weighting. For example, more weight could be assigned to decisions that have a symbolic importance, that demonstrate more clearly than others the policymaking powers of the level which takes them.

These systems of weighting were tested. In particular, the importance of the various levels in the decision-making structure for public education in the 14 countries as a whole was calculated using in turn the six systems of weighting. Table 3 gives the minimum and maximum values obtained for each level.

The differences between the extreme values obtained are small in the case of central government and Level UI, and slightly larger for the school and Level LI, but without this causing any major change in the configuration of the decision-making structure. The ranking of the levels within the structure, for example, is not affected.

Comparing this table with the results of the "weighting" finally adopted (Table 5, Part II), it will be seen however that the latter tends somewhat to reduce the importance of the school and increase that of Level LI. In other words, decisions generally taken by Level LI were considered somewhat less important than those taken by the school when the different weighting systems (2, 3, 4 and 5) were compiled.

Can these different weighting systems change the position of a country in relation to the others? Table 4 provides an answer as regards the proportion of decisions taken by the school at ISCED stage II Public. The answer is yes, but this change is never likely to alter radically the perception of the school's autonomy within a country. Nowhere is the degree of school autonomy rated as low by one system of weighting and as moderate or high by another. However, it can be seen that countries, which in any case are close to one another, swap or change their respective positions. For example, under the weighting systems 1, 4 and 6, French and German schools have an almost identical degree of

Table 3. **Importance of the different levels depending on the system of weighting used (Public)**

	School		Level LI		Level UI		Central gov.	
	Min.	Max.	Min.	Max.	Min.	Max.	Min.	Max.
ISCED 1*	35	43	25	36	10	10	19	23*
ISCED 2	38	44	23	32	11	13	19	21
ISCED 3	40	46	15	20	18	21	19	21

* The minimum and maximum figures in a row do not total 100 because these figures may be taken from different systems of weighting.

Table 4. **Importance of the school in the decision-making process depending on the system of weighting used (ISCED 2, Public)**

	Weighting						Max. diff.
	1	2	3	4	5	6	
Austria	38	37	44	44	44	36	8
Belgium	25	27	30	27	31	23	8
Denmark	41	42	51	46	52	39	13
Finland	40	43	46	39	48	38	10
France	31	31	35	34	36	30	6
Germany	33	36	40	36	41	30	11
Ireland	73	73	74	73	75	72	3
New Zealand	71	78	79	79	76	77	8
Norway	32	30	35	32	39	27	12
Portugal	40	37	41	39	40	41	4
Spain	28	31	36	36	35	27	9
Sweden	48	47	55	52	56	47	9
Switzerland	10	10	16	14	14	11	6
United States	26	28	34	31	36	25	11
Total	38	39	44	42	44	38	

autonomy whereas, under systems 2, 3 and 5, German schools are rated as slightly more autonomous (by five percentage points) than their French counterparts.

The difference between the school's powers under the most and the least "generous" weighting system is less than 10 points in nine out of the 14 countries, and between 10 and 13 points in the remaining five (Denmark, Finland, Germany, Norway, United States).

What this seems to suggest is that a weighting system other than the one adopted would not improve the comparison in any real way unless it were based on principles that had been clearly identified and were logically related to the recognised major objectives of education systems in general.

In relation to the "weighting" system that was finally adopted, a difference of less than 4 points between two situations (*e.g.* between the importance of the school in the decision-making structures of two countries) represents only one decision, while even a difference of four points is likely to represent one rather than two decisions. Consequently, when comparing two countries, the principle we endeavoured to apply was to consider as significant only differences of five or more points, since this would obviously mean a difference of at least two decisions. When it came to comparing the overall situation for all 14 countries combined – for example, between ISCED 1 and ISCED 2, or between public and private – it was considered that differences of two points or more could be meaningful.

Implementation

Collecting the data

A pilot questionnaire was compiled during the summer of 1990 to which 7 countries replied: England, France, Portugal, Scotland, Sweden, Switzerland and the United States. The main problems occurred with the definitions of the ISCED levels, the aggregations (in the case of federal countries) and the definitions of certain items.

The results of this phase were presented to the meeting of Network C of the OECD/CERI International Indicators of Education Systems project held in Avignon (France) in April 1991.

At the same time, an improved questionnaire was sent to all the countries belonging to the network. The results of this phase were presented to the General Assembly of the OECD/CERI/INES project at Lugano (Switzerland) in September 1991, and were subsequently incorporated in the form of five indicators in *Education at a Glance* (OECD, 1992).

Following this presentation it was decided, firstly, to compile this report and, secondly, to invite countries that were not members of Network C to reply to the questionnaire – which a few did during the early part of 1992.

A preliminary version of this report was submitted to a peripheral meeting of respondents at the time of the November 1992 meeting of Network C at the Hague (Netherlands). It was decided on this occasion to set up a verification procedure to check the data that had been collected.

The reason for this was that, during the first phase, the procedures adopted for filling in the initial questionnaires sometimes differed from one country to another, while for certain questions the definitions had raised problems. What is more, the information (covering 1988) was becoming outdated.

In order to remedy these shortcomings the plan was, as part of this verification procedure, to re-emphasize the importance of the study, specify exactly how the questionnaires should be filled in, clarify the definitions supplied in the case of certain questions and collect certain additional information (*e.g.* the number of pupils concerned, the names given to the intermediate levels, the names of team members, etc.). The main phases in the procedure were as follows.

The national co-ordinator was asked to set up two teams to verify or fill in the questionnaires. One of the two teams had to comprise those persons who had replied to the initial questionnaires and their task was to check the earlier replies and make sure that they corresponded to the new instructions. The second team had to fill in a fresh set of questionnaires. The co-ordinator took the two sets of replies and, together with the team leaders, looked into any discrepancies there might be in order to iron these out; he noted these discrepancies on a concordance sheet together with the solutions that had been found. The replies to the questionnaires therefore included details of any differences of view between the two teams responsible for these.

31

In some countries, more than two teams were set up to reply to the questionnaires and deal with, for example, the different educational stages or the public and private sectors.

Although the verification procedure was compulsory, countries were offered two alternatives: in order that the data should be considered for publication, countries had either to comply with the verification procedure or confirm officially in writing the replies provided initially. For example, no data are published herein for Italy, since it neither carried out the verification procedure nor provided any official confirmation of the information it had originally submitted. Germany, on the other hand, is included in this analysis since, although it decided it was unnecessary to apply the verification procedure, it did confirm in writing the accuracy of the information originally supplied.

The verification procedure proved to be very worthwhile. It helped to ensure more accurate interpretation of the data, increase its comparability, remove the ambiguity of certain replies, optimise the response rate and generate additional information.

It goes without saying that the reliability of the data used depends entirely on the meticulousness and care taken by the national working groups in answering the questionnaires. Judging by the numerous annotations and comments accompanying their replies, and the differences of opinion or doubts to which attention was drawn, the work of these groups can be considered both conscientious and thorough.

The countries were asked to send the results of their verification by 15 February 1993 at the latest. On the basis of these data the four indicators on decision-making processes included in *Education at a Glance* (OECD, 1993) were calculated. In some cases, the values for these indicators differ slightly from those published herein, the reason for this being that it proved impossible to resolve the problem regarding decision S2 in time for this second edition of *Education at a Glance*.

A preliminary version of this report, based on the above data, was presented to a peripheral meeting of respondents at the time of the main meeting of Network C in Paris in June 1993. The extremely useful comments that were made by Member countries on this occasion were considered and discussed during the second half of 1993 and have resulted in the present text.

In the case of a study that is as experimental in character as this one, it is not surprising that even after compiling three successive sets of information – each taking into account the errors noted in the previous ones – a number of problems remained, of which only some have been resolved here.

Some unresolved difficulties

Responses to decision S2 (creation and suppression of classes) were excluded from the data for all countries because of an ambiguity in the English translation of this decision, which meant that the English and the French-speaking respondents were not answering the same question.[3] The effect of this was to reduce the total number of decisions analysed to 34 and to increase slightly the weight of the other decisions in the field "Planning and Structures", each of which now represents 3.6 per cent of the overall decision-making structure.

It ought also perhaps to have been specified whether teachers' "career" (R4-2) meant within and/or outside the teaching profession. Another decision occasionally caused some misunderstanding: methods of grouping pupils (P5) was understood, by one country at least, as meaning the possibility of creating larger or smaller groups, whereas what was meant was the decision as to the principle to be used in setting up such groups (random choice, age, level, sex, courses followed, etc.).

Judging by the annotations accompanying the replies, some of the instructions regarding modes of decision-making also proved difficult to understand.

The idea of decisions taken in conjunction with another body raised a number of problems that were easy to solve, whereas that of a "set framework" raised some that were more tricky.

According to the instructions, this applied solely to decisions that are taken by two levels within the structure in conjunction with one another. This meant, therefore, that if a decision is taken at national level by the central administration in conjunction with, for instance, the national teachers' unions, then this could be considered as an autonomous decision (A) by the national level.

For example, Denmark, when it states that the school takes the decision regarding a pupil's streaming autonomously (A), noting however "with the parents' agreement", was replying correctly to the questionnaire, but those countries that did not give a reply for a particular decision because it is decided by "joint negotiation" should have put an "A" against the level where this negotiation takes place.

Moreover, it may be the case that the level "consulted" has in reality a substantial influence on the decision: one of the inherent limitations of this study is that it focuses on the decision-making processes as prescribed in the legislation and regulations, and not on the importance in practice of the actors involved. Nevertheless, although respondents were asked to indicate whether reality differed considerably from the prescribed procedure, they did so only to a very limited extent. While it is frequently noted that the situation as described does not apply to certain areas or to certain experimental schools, there is rarely any mention of deviations from the actual, officially prescribed procedure. Only in the case of Sweden is there mention of a "tendency towards greater autonomy for schools" in connection with the powers officially assigned to the lower intermediate level (Kommun) with regard, for example, to the choice of a school (P1) and the use of resources intended for capital expenditure (F2-2). This note also mentions that the legislation is going to be amended and that this is being anticipated by what is actually happening on the ground.

Countries sometimes found it difficult to decide whether a decision was taken autonomously or within a set framework. In this respect, the two groups in the United States differed on how to answer P1 (the choice of school in the case of public education): should they put an "A" or a "C" against LI? Their Chairman was called upon to cast the deciding vote.

France had similar doubts about the same question with regard to ISCED 1. During the course of the verification procedure it substituted an "A" for a "C" for the level LI, considering that in the end the legal framework imposed on the communes in this respect was not very restrictive. Likewise, Norway felt that the ban imposed by national legislation on grouping pupils in accordance with their standard did not mean that in all other respects the school could be considered as able to decide autonomously on how its pupils should be grouped (P5). Perhaps a country where such a ban might be less easily accepted and respected would have been more inclined to state that the school's decision is taken within a framework set by central government.

Similar doubts can occur even as regards the level at which a decision is positioned. In the case of S4 (choice of range of subject matters) France put an "A" in the column "Central government", despite the fact that colleges (ISCED 2, Public) can have a say as to the choice that will be offered to pupils with respect to a second modern language. However, it was felt that this freedom of action was so slight as not to justify attributing the decision to the school within a framework set at national level.

This example, coupled with the contrasting one of Norway in the case of P5, shows that in reality there is a continuous progression from a decision taken autonomously by a higher level:

- a decision taken autonomously by the higher level;
- a trifling degree of autonomy conceded to the lower level;
- a decision taken by the lower level within a rigid framework set by the higher level;
- a decision taken by the lower level within a far from rigid framework set by the higher level; and
- a decision taken completely autonomously by the lower level.

Difficulties such as these can be resolved only by means of a common conception among the respondents from the different countries as to what is trifling, what is too flexible to be called a framework, etc. It would seem that a similarity of views in this respect was fairly widespread among respondents, and the comparison of situations and replies should help to improve this situation.

Part II
Results

A distinction is usually drawn between centralised education systems in which a Ministry of Education is in full control, and decentralised systems in which the main responsibilities are held by local authorities. France and the United Kingdom are often quoted as prime examples of these two different categories.

In the mid-1970s this distinction was still valid. In addition to France, the countries that could be placed in the first category were Italy, Portugal, Spain and Sweden, while in addition to the UK, those falling into the second were Canada, the Netherlands, Switzerland and the United States.

Holmes (1979), on the basis of data assembled by UNESCO, draws a distinction between countries whose education system is managed and administered mainly at the national, regional or local level.

Over the last 15 years the decision-making structure in education systems has changed, in many cases radically. These changes have been accompanied by debates, often very lively ones, on what should be the appropriate degree of decentralisation. The reports commissioned by the OECD on the education policies of certain countries are a good source of information on the arguments used in this respect.

These have to do with the consequences of the decision-making process in four respects: for democracy, for equality of opportunity, for the system's capacity to adapt and, lastly, for its capacity to be governed.

Some consider that decentralisation fosters democracy by bringing the decision-making centres closer to the citizens, who are thus able to participate and to control them more effectively.[4] The argument here is that decentralisation gives more powers to the citizens themselves.

Others, or even the same persons, consider that decentralisation is necessary because "it is increasingly difficult, if not impossible, to control complex modern education systems from a single centre"(OECD, 1986, p. 23). What is being sought in this case is a decentralised model capable of taking the place of a poorly functioning system of control at national level.

In the first of these arguments, the emphasis is on the control that individuals would be able to exercise on bodies that are closer to them; in the second, the emphasis is placed on the control that these less remote bodies would be able to exercise on individuals.

Although the thrust of these two arguments is different, they are nevertheless not contradictory in that it is easy to imagine citizens exercising close control over local authorities which, in turn, closely control the actors within the education system itself. In this respect, advocates of centralisation are likely to highlight the risks of local control over these professionals or to claim that the concern for democracy is no more than a screen for a desire for management control.

It is generally acknowledged that, with decentralisation, the pupils within the different geographical units to which powers are devolved are more likely to find themselves with unequal chances of access to education services, or with unequal chances of receiving an education of a high standard.

Since the poorest of the geographical units are obviously those where there is the highest proportion of poor individuals, this geographical inequality is also, and above all, a social inequality. In fact, it is often the case, in decentralised systems, that the central authority has to take charge of some of the programmes that are targeted to disadvantaged children – as in the United States, for example. Supporters of centralisation argue that this type of ex post facto measure leads to more inequalities than a system which places all individuals on an equal footing at the outset. To which supporters of decentralisation will retort that centralised systems themselves are not without inequalities.

Another line of argument is that decentralised decisions are more adapted to local realities – and particularly to the employment situation – and that it has become more important than ever to ensure this adaptation, either because these realities have become more diverse or because each of them has become more complex to deal with. It has also been claimed that more autonomy has been granted to secondary schools in France since 1970 for a reason of this kind: "Once schools, the teaching staff and pupils start to become increasingly heterogeneous, decisions have to be devolved to smaller units where closer knowledge of one another means that differences are more readily taken into account, at least intuitively"(Derouet, 1987). Centralised bureaucracies, although often considered as "competent", are criticised for "their lack of imagination, their top-heavy structure and their affection for red tape"(OECD, 1986, p. 24). By contrast, a decentralised system is seen as favouring "emulation, rapidity of decision-making in the field, innovation on the part of actors free to tackle the problems as they arise and the flexibility associated with direct information on events"(OECD, 1991b, p. 64).

However, OECD examiners are also obliged to acknowledge that decentralised systems have certain rigidities and that it is difficult to bring about certain overall and clearly necessary changes therein. Some see this as a direct outcome of decentralisation. It is considered that centralised systems adapt less readily to spatial differences but more readily to temporal changes in the environment. "The structure (of the German school system) is somewhat traditional and resembles to a large extent the erstwhile structure of the French school system. This is one of the consequences of federalism because, in order to secure any fundamental change, all of the partners would have to agree to it"(Kodron and Huck, 1993, p. 20).

Yet this conservatism can be considered as an advantage, because it permits the preservation of differences "in a world which tends to standardise many spheres of social life through the influence of economic forces and the media".[5] But it can also be considered as a drawback, on the grounds that, while decentralisation may undoubtedly preserve certain traditional and possibly worthwhile differences, it also generates differences that are less worthwhile in order to justify the existence of each of its component units. "The very close contact with reality and the great freedom of decision that seem to go hand-in-hand with decentralisation may be factors making for rigidity, protection of what is believed to be an identity and for conservatism vis-à-vis the realities on the basis of which the actors legitimate their own form of existence. The diversity of systems, instead of leading to emulation, may go together with mutual observation marked by rigidifying distrust rather than dynamising competition"(OECD, 1991*b*, p. 64). It should however be said that this idea runs counter to another, propounded for example by Archer (1984) in a comparison of the French and English education systems, whereby centralised systems "are characterised by alternating long periods of quiescence and short periods of crisis" whereas, in decentralised systems, change is seen as being "constantly initiated, revised and challenged at various levels: the school, the local community, the nation (...)" (Bellat and van Zanten, 1992, p. 20). According to the first of these arguments, decentralisation makes change more difficult, according to the second it makes it less abrupt, more continuous.

A system's ability to adapt to its environment – to spatial disparities as well as temporal changes – is one of the factors that determine its effectiveness. But its effectiveness may also depend on the personal and untrammelled will of those in charge of it or the actors involved. Here again, there are arguments on either side.

Some contend that it is at the level of the schools that decisions are best taken, because it is at this level that users can exert effective pressure, because extensive autonomy allows competition, which is both a regulating mechanism and an incentive to improve performance.

However, it has also been claimed that it can be shown that the effect of education on economic growth has been more marked in countries where the decision-making processes were more heavily concentrated at the national level (France prior to 1970) or at the regional level (Germany) than in countries where the education system was more decentralised (United States) (see Garnier *et al.*, 1989). What these authors contend is that countries with a less decentralised system are more able to promote forms of education suited to the needs of the economy – technical education, for example – while at the same time maintaining the quality of this education. It is considered that one reason why quality has been maintained is the fact that teachers have been able to maintain high expectations for all of the pupils. Furthermore, the authors also argue that national qualifications provide employers with a clearer idea of an individual's skills. The intervention of users, and parents in particular, is therefore considered as being in some cases conducive to effectiveness and, in others, not.

The debate about the decentralisation of education systems therefore involves a number of fundamental values, concerning moreover several aspects of this issue. The arguments put forward by either side strongly suggest that the optimum solution is to be found in a form of articulation between centralisation and decentralisation. For example, the OECD examiners who analysed Norway's system of education, although favourably impressed by the decentralisation that had been carried out, observed that "What is, however, missing is the belief that with decentralisation the centre should not abandon its role but must find a new one [whereby] the centre gains in influence at the same time as it relinquishes its formal powers'' (OECD, 1990a, p.18).

This comment highlights one of the limitations of this study, namely that the influence, the power of a level within the education system does not depend solely on the proportion of decisions it takes. It is clear, for example, that the Federal Department of Education in Washington, through the publication of analyses and objectives, has an influence on the US system of education which falls well outside the scope of what we shall be measuring here.

But the idea of an articulation between powers at the local and national level also demonstrates why it is necessary to determine more precisely the decision-making structures within the different countries: the debate, as well as the decision-making process, can no longer confine itself to what has become an unduly simplistic opposition between centralised and decentralised systems. We must at least be able to determine in what field, at what level and in what way a country takes its decisions. The results set out hereunder represent a first step in this direction. They are presented in the following way:

The first section discusses in general terms the respective roles of the different *levels* in the decision-making process. The decisions are then analysed in greater detail in the subsequent three sections, the first dealing with the *modes* of decision-making, the second combining *modes* and *levels*, and the third analysing these in conjunction with the *fields* in which these decisions are taken.

The results are presented systematically in each section: the picture obtained from aggregation of the data for each country is described and then the differences between countries are discussed. These differences are treated in two ways: descriptively (identification of groups of homogeneous countries, or ''models'') and analytically (establishment of any logical relationship between the existence or absence of certain characteristics).

In both cases – general description and analysis of differences – we examine public education and then private education and, in both sectors, the situation in lower secondary education (ISCED 2), and then in the other two levels of education (ISCED 1 – primary education, and ISCED 3 – upper secondary education).

Levels of decision-making

The overall picture

For the period when the analysis was carried out, the picture that was revealed by aggregating the data for the different education systems was, in the case of public lower secondary education, as follows: the school takes a good third of decisions and the level immediately above (LI) just short of a third, while a fifth of decisions are taken at the highest level. The share for the upper intermediate level (UI) is low: it has to be borne in mind that education systems often comprise only three tiers (see Table 5).

Table 5. **Decision-making levels in a number of OECD countries taken together**[1]

	No.[2]	School	Lower intermediate level (LI)	Upper intermediate level (UI)	Central gov.
Public sector					
ISCED 1	14	35[3]	35	10	20
ISCED 2	14	38	31	12	19
ISCED 3	14	41	19	21	19
Private sector					
ISCED 1	5	75	4	8	13
ISCED 2	6	75	3	9	13
ISCED 3	6	76	2	10	13

1. Unless otherwise indicated, all of the figures in the tables in this study denote the percentage of decisions taken at a given level and/or in the manner indicated.
2. Number of countries in the combined total. If a level does not exist in a particular country, it is nonetheless taken into account by considering that no decision is taken at that level. The importance of a level thus depends also on the number of countries where it exists. Each country has been assigned the same weight.
3. Of the 34 decisions studied, in the case of primary education (ISCED 1) for all of the 14 countries combined, 35 per cent were taken at the level of the school in 1990/91.

The pattern for the other two stages of public education is not basically different: the school is still the level where most decisions are taken and the importance of the top level is much the same. However, there are one or two notable differences: schools exercise somewhat more power at the higher stages of education, while level LI is of less importance in the case of these higher stages of education; some of this it loses to the school of course, but most to the upper intermediate level whose importance increases in the case of upper secondary education (ISCED 3).

Private education is sufficiently important to appear in the study in only six countries (Austria, Belgium, France, Spain, Portugal, United States) out of the 14. There are no differences between the three stages of education, with the pattern throughout being fairly straightforward: three out of four decisions are taken at school level (or roughly twice as many as in the public sector), while level LI is virtually absent from the structure and neither of the other two levels accounts for even 15 per cent of decisions.[6]

It is therefore clear that the powers of schools are generally much greater in private education. It is also to be noted, however, that these greater powers are to the detriment of the level immediately above the school: in the case of ISCED 1 and ISCED 2 in particular, the combined importance of the school plus LI is comparable (70/79; 69/78) for both the public and the private sector.

Country comparison

Public sector, ISCED 2

Decision-making processes differ considerably from country to country. There is no one model or even one that would apply to the vast majority of countries with only a few exceptions (Table 6).

Countries can be classified in a number of ways on the basis of these figures. Countries where powers at national level are nil or limited (less than 11 per cent of decisions) can be distinguished from those where they are greater (from 14 to 33 per cent of decisions). The first of these groups consists of the United States, Switzerland and Belgium, where powers at national level are nil, and Germany and Sweden where they are very limited. The second group comprises Austria, Denmark, Spain, Finland, France, Ireland, Norway and New Zealand. Only in Portugal does the central level have substantial powers (57 per cent).

The biggest countries or those with the largest populations might be expected to be those with the fewest powers at national level, which would avoid decisions being too far removed from users. However, this is not the case, since both small and large countries are found in each of the two groups.

On the basis of the importance of the school in the decision-making structure, the countries divide into six groups:

1. Ireland, New Zealand (73 and 71 per cent respectively);
2. Sweden (48 per cent);

Table 6. **Decision-making levels in 14 OECD countries (ISCED 2, Public)** [1]

	School	Lower intermediate level (LI)	Upper intermediate level (UI)	Central gov.
Austria	28	8	26	28
Belgium	25	50	25	
Denmark	41	44		15
Finland	40	47		13
France	31		36	33
Germany	33	42	18	7
Ireland	73	8		19
New Zealand	71			29
Norway	32	45		23
Portugal	40		3	57
Spain	28	26	13	33
Sweden	48	48		4
Switzerland	10	40	50	
United States	26	71	3	

1. In the German educational system, 33 per cent of the decisions studied are taken by schools, either autonomously, in conjunction with another level in the system, or within a framework set by a higher authority.

3. Austria, Denmark, Finland, Portugal (38-41 per cent);
4. Germany, France, Norway (31-33 per cent);
5. Belgium, Spain, United States (25-28 per cent);
6. Switzerland (10 per cent).

In Ireland and New Zealand, the school's importance in the decision-making structure is similar to that for private education. In Ireland's case this is partly due to the fact that public sector schools belong to religious establishments, which enjoy a broad measure of autonomy as regards resources and management of non-teaching staff. In the vast majority of the countries studied, the school takes between 25 and 41 per cent of decisions.

Another distinction that can be made is that between countries where one level is predominant and others where powers are more evenly divided between several levels.

In a system where all four levels were of equal importance, each would take 25 per cent of the decisions. One could therefore describe a structure as having a single dominant level when one of these takes over 50 per cent of the decisions, as having two dominant levels when these two together take over 75 per cent of the decisions with neither of them alone accounting for more than 50 per cent, and as being a multi-level structure in all other cases (see Table 7).

This typology highlights the wide diversity of situations: not only are there systems with one, two or three dominant levels, but also where the single dominant level can be either the school, the local level (LI) or the national level.

None of the models (A, B or C) in this classification accounts for a majority of the 14 countries.

It is possible that the origin of some of these structural similarities is cultural, in the Nordic countries for example, but this is not generally the case. It is unlikely, for instance, that the reasons for the autonomy of New Zealand's schools and those of Ireland are the same.

It would seem therefore that the way public education is organised is primarily a reflection of the diversity of countries' political history, even though they may have begun to move in similar directions in recent years, for example towards granting greater powers to schools.

Table 7. **Education systems by main decision-making level (ISCED 2, Public)**

A. Systems with a single dominant level	– School: Ireland, New Zealand – Local (LI): Belgium, United States – Central gov.: Portugal
B. Systems with two dominant levels	– School and Local (LI): Denmark, Finland, Germany, Norway, Sweden, Switzerland
C. Multi-level systems	– Austria, France, Spain

However, taking those countries where either the school, the local level or the two combined predominate, these make up a majority of 10 out of the total of 14. It can therefore said that, in the countries studied, decentralised models are more common than centralised models.

Among these decentralised systems, some have become so only recently while others are long established. Presumably, the reason for the change in the first case was to achieve greater effectiveness. The structures in countries like Germany, the United States and Ireland date back to a time when this concern – widespread but nevertheless recent – did not exist. A concern for effectiveness is therefore not likely to have been the main motive for decentralisation in their case, although it is probably safe to assume that, in countries like the United States for example, it was already a widely held belief that nothing highly centralised would ever work properly.

It is very likely, therefore, that membership of this group of countries is governed by two principles: one would be the idea of bringing decisions closer to users in the hope of making these are relevant as possible to the differing local situations or of generating more pressure from quality-conscious users. The other would be the desire to establish a firm foundation within the local community, the size of which might in some cases be considerable. Lastly, the difference should be noted between systems that bring into play a specialised local education authority (the district in the United States, for example) and those where education is simply one of the many responsibilities of the traditional local authority.

The multi-level group of countries, although smaller, is fairly heterogeneous, firstly because the intermediate level can be either the first (Spain) or the second (Austria, France) and secondly because, in Spain, the 1990/91 structure was one that existed during the transition from a centralised model to one where the "autonomous regions" (UI) were to see their powers substantially increased.

Looking at this classification, it is clear that the formerly centralised countries have all undertaken some degree of decentralisation, albeit in different ways. France has moved towards a system where the school, the regional and academy levels (UI) and central government share decision-making powers more or less equally. Spain is moving towards a system where the three lower levels will take virtually all of the decisions. In the Nordic countries these powers are split between the schools and the local authorities. Portugal has simply increased the powers of its schools.

Apart from this classification by country, is it possible to work out any rules regarding the respective importance of the various decision-making levels? The answer seems to be yes, at least for this sample of countries.

This is apparent from Table 8 which shows the coefficients of correlation between the proportion of decisions taken by the various levels in the 14 countries as a whole, notwithstanding the smallness of this sample and notwithstanding the fact that the variables concerned are not independent of one another.

In this case, therefore, one needs to bear in mind the meaningfulness of the correlations observed. However, even with this caviat, the table reveals some interesting information.

When many decisions are taken at the intermediate levels (LI and/or UI), few are taken at the national level and vice-versa. There is nothing surprising about this, since the alternative to decision-making at these two levels is obvious.

The other finding is more unexpected (see Table 8): when many decisions are taken at the intermediate levels, the schools take few. These negative correlations between the importance of the intermediate levels and that of the school are not borne out between the national level and the school level or, at least, are much weaker (-0.11 as compared with -0.75). In other words, an important national level does not necessarily imply that the school has no autonomy. To some extent, this is not surprising. These are the two levels furthest removed from one another. On account of this, it is logical that they should exercise their powers in distinct areas. However, the persistence of the "centralised" model in which central government exercised all the powers, including at the expense of the school, has meant that this logic has tended to be forgotten.

The negative correlation between the powers of the intermediate levels and those of the school can be illustrated by referring to Table 6. In the four countries where the national level is particularly powerful (Portugal, New Zealand, Spain, France), the school represents on average 42 per cent of the decision-making structure. In the four countries where the local level (LI) is particularly powerful (United States, Belgium, Sweden, Finland), it represents 35 per cent of this structure, *i.e.* between two and four decisions fewer. In the four countries where the regional level (UI) is particularly powerful (Austria, Belgium, France, Switzerland), the school represents 26 per cent of the decision-making structure, *i.e.* between four and seven decisions fewer than in the first case.

This finding obviously does not rule out the possibility of having a system in which the intermediate levels as well as the schools have extensive powers. This is the case at present in the Nordic countries. Given the current state of education systems, another theory would seem to be more plausible, but this is all supposition. One such supposition

Table 8. **Correlations between the importance of the different decision-making levels**[1]

	School	LI	UI	LI or UI	Central gov.
School	1	−0.48	−0.61	−0.75*	−0.11
LI	−0.48	1	−0.33	−	−0.62
UI	−0.61	−0.33	1	−	−0.45
LI or UI	−0.75*	−	−	1	−0.71**
Central gov.	−0.11	−0.51	−0.45	−0.71**	1

* Significant at 99%.
** Significant at 95%.
1. Among the 14 countries studied, the coefficient of correlation between the importance of the school and that of level LI in the decision-making structure is -0.48. This coefficient would be equal to zero if one level's importance was independent of another's. When it is negative, this is because the more powers one level has, the fewer the other tends to have. Since the correlation was calculated on the basis of a very small number of observations, its value has to be high in order to be statistically significant.

might be that, precisely because the intermediate levels are closer to the school, they can to some extent take decisions in its place.

Another supposition, based on historical circumstances, is that it was easier for centralised systems (France, Spain, Portugal, Sweden) to delegate authority for some decisions to the schools than it was for systems where the power was vested more in the regional or local levels (United States, Germany, Switzerland) to secure the necessary consensus for a reform of this type. The data analysed herein tend to confirm these suppositions and the similar conclusions that were put forward in Part I.

This does not mean that decision-making structures in the so called ''decentralised'' countries have not evolved. In certain cases, some of the regional levels have granted more autonomy to schools and, in others, some of the decision-making levels have made fuller use of the powers that they possess. An example of this is the United States, where the federal government has recently increased its influence over the system through the publication of reports such as *A Nation at Risk* and by organising a meeting of governors at which it proposed six ''goals'' for the education system for the year 2000. Likewise, the individual states in the US have indirectly influenced the decision-making process through their efforts to secure the adoption of standards and systems of evaluation. The survey method we used is clearly not able to identify changes of this kind but, on the other hand, it does show that centralised systems are not the inflexible, hidebound monsters that they are sometimes made out to be.

It should however be borne in mind that, in this instance, we have not taken into account the modes of decision-making. It is easier for decision-making levels close to the school to take decisions in consultation with it. For example, ISCED level 2 public schools in the United States are usually consulted by the district about the recruitment of teaching and non-teaching staff and their working conditions. The range of subjects taught by these schools is also decided in conjunction with the district. Similarly, in Switzerland, the canton takes decisions in conjunction with the school concerning school textbooks, pupil guidance and counselling, and the use of operating funds.

It must also be remembered that, for the reasons that were stated earlier, this study does not distinguish between a decentralised agency of central government and an elected local body. It therefore does not cover all of the criteria which determine the ''central-ised'' or ''decentralised'' character of an education system.

We shall now be looking at whether these results with regard to ISCED 2 also hold true for the other levels of public education.

Public sector, ISCED 1 and 3

The data have been analysed in order to determine whether the decision-making structure varied or, to be more precise, whether the different levels had the same importance for each of the ISCED stages of education. Considering the two intermediate levels as one, and thus ignoring any possible transfers of powers between levels LI and UI, there were three models that emerged.

In model 1, the importance of each level remains the same, or virtually the same, for each ISCED stage. This we can call model xxx: the decision-making structure is exactly

44

the same for all three ISCED stages in the case of Germany, the United States and Sweden, and virtually the same[7] in Belgium and Spain.

In model 2, the decision-making structure is the same for ISCED 1 and ISCED 2, but different for ISCED 3. This model, which we can call xxy, applies to Austria, Denmark, Norway, New Zealand and Switzerland, while the situation in Finland is very similar.

In model 3, ISCED 2 and ISCED 3 have the same decision-making structure, and it is ISCED 1 that differs. This model we can call xyy and it applies in France, Ireland and Portugal. It should be mentioned that, in Portugal, primary education (ISCED 1) is split into two phases, the first of which lasts four years and has its own specific decision-making structure, whereas the second, which lasts two years, has the same structure as ISCED 2 and 3.

It is interesting to note that model xxy is more common than model xyy. As far as the decision-making structure is concerned, the dividing line – when there is one – is more often between the two stages of secondary education than between primary and secondary.

From Table 9, in which levels LI and UI are combined, it will be seen that two countries classified as model xxy (Denmark and Switzerland) revert to the general pattern, i.e. at ISCED 3 greater powers are vested in the school and in the national level to the detriment of the intermediate levels. In the other countries classified as having this model (Austria, Finland, New Zealand, Norway) it will also be seen that – except for Norway – more powers are exercised by schools at ISCED 3, but not necessarily by the national level.

Table 9.   **Decision-making levels for the three stages of public education in 14 OECD countries**

	School			Intermediate levels (LI + UI)			Central government		
	ISCED 1	ISCED 2	ISCED 3	ISCED 1	ISCED 2	ISCED 3	ISCED 1	ISCED 2	ISCED 3
Austria	38	38	42	35	35	35	27	27	22
Belgium	28	25	25	72	75	75	0	0	0
Denmark	41	41	43	44	44	32	15	15	25
Finland	43	40	60	47	47	28	10	13	12
France	17	31	31	51	36	38	32	33	30
Germany	32	32	32	61	61	61	7	7	7
Ireland	50	73	73	0	8	8	50	19	19
New Zealand	71	71	79	0	0	0	29	29	21
Norway	32	32	26	45	45	52	23	23	22
Portugal	31	40	40	21	3	3	48	57	57
Spain	28	28	28	39	39	35	33	33	37
Sweden	48	48	48	48	48	48	4	4	4
Switzerland	10	10	21	90	90	68	0	0	11
United States	26	26	26	74	74	74	0	0	0

In Switzerland, the level closest to the school (LI) gradually loses its powers until it has none in ISCED 3.

In model xyy countries – France, Ireland and Portugal – schools in ISCED levels 2 and 3 have more powers than those in ISCED 1.

In fact, the general trend observed for the countries as a whole (*i.e.* an increase in the powers of the school and a decrease in those of the intermediate levels as one moves up from ISCED 1 to ISCED 3) holds true for most countries except for a few fairly minor exceptions:

– In Ireland, an intermediate level takes a few decisions at ISCED 2 and 3, whereas primary education is governed solely by the two levels at either extreme.
– In Norway, schools at upper secondary level (ISCED 3) have somewhat less autonomy than their counterparts in ISCED 1 and 2. The national level keeps a fairly tight control over ISCED 3 [its courses (S5) for example]. But, more particularly, the *Fylkesskole styret* (UI), which intervenes at ISCED 3, takes slightly more decisions – 18 as compared with 16 – than does the *Skolestyret* (LI) which intervenes at ISCED 1 and 2.
– In Austria, ISCED 3 schools are somewhat less independent than their counter-parts in ISCED 1 and 2, but the national level intervenes to a lesser extent than the intermediate levels at ISCED 3.

A level can have the same importance in the decision-making structures of two stages of education, yet without taking the same decisions in both cases. In order that the decision-making process should be the same for two stages of education, not only must the same decisions be taken at the same level but also in the same mode. This can be considered to be the case whenever a particular country has filled in a single question-naire for more than one stage of education. On the basis of this criterion, the countries concerned are as follows:

– in model xxx: Germany, United States, Sweden;
– in model xxy: Denmark, Spain, Norway, New Zealand;
– in model xyy: Belgium, Ireland.

Using this criterion, it is nonetheless still true that the difference, where there is one, is more often between the pattern for ISCED 1 and 2 and that for ISCED 3 than between the pattern for ISCED 1 and that for ISCED 2 and 3. By and large, this means that the difference occurs more frequently between compulsory and non-compulsory education than between primary and secondary education.

In the case of eight of the 14 countries, the classification of education systems (Table 10) for ISCED 2 (Table 9) remains unchanged for the other stages of education.

The deviations that occur are as follows:

– In primary education, it is less common than in ISCED 2 to find systems where there is one dominant level. For example, in the case of primary education, Portugal and Switzerland come under the group of countries with two main levels.

Table 10. **Education systems according to the dominant levels
in their decision-making structure (Public)** [1]

ISCED 2		ISCED 1	ISCED 3
	Systems with one dominant level		
IRE, NZL	School	– IRE	
BEL, USA	Local (LI)		
SWI	Regional (UI)	– SWI	
POR	Central government	+ IRE, – POR	
	Systems with two dominant levels		
GER, DEN, FIN,	School and Local (LI)		- DEN, NOR
NOR, SWE	School and Regional (UI)		+ DEN, NOR
	School and Central gov.	+ POR	
	Local (LI) and Regional (UI)	+ SWI	
OST, SPA, FRA	*Systems with three levels*		

1. This table shows the differences between the decision-making structure for ISCED stages 1 and 3 and that for ISCED 2.
Where the situation for ISCED 2 also applies at ISCED 1 and 3, country names are not repeated in these last two columns.
For example, the school is the dominant level in Ireland for ISCED 2 and for ISCED 3, but it is central government in the
case of ISCED 1.

- In Denmark and Norway, in the case of secondary education, the local level (LI)
  has no powers as regards upper secondary (ISCED 3) whereas it has as regards
  lower secondary (ISCED 2).
- In the case of primary education, there are seven countries with systems with two
  dominant levels. However, depending on the country, these two levels can be any
  of four "pairings" out of the possible total of six. The variety of ways in which
  public education systems are organised is no less great for ISCED 1 (and 3) than
  for ISCED 2.

Private sector, ISCED 1, 2, 3

The importance of the three decision-making levels in private education systems is
shown in Table 11 (see "Methods", Part I).

The overall model defined above for private education was that three out of four
decisions are taken by the school, with none of the other levels, either central government
or indeed the two intermediate levels combined – accounting for even 15 per cent of the
decisions. Private sector structures, nonetheless, differ quite considerably from one country to another.

What the countries have in common, however, is the *school's* high degree of
autonomy. There are countries where the private school takes more than 80 per cent of
the decisions concerning it (United States, Portugal) and those where it takes "only"
about 60-70 per cent (Belgium, Spain, France). One can scarcely therefore call these

Table 11. **Decision-making levels in the three stages of private education in six OECD countries**[1]

	% pupils in private sector	School			Intermediate levels (LI + UI)			Central government		
		ISCED 1	ISCED 2	ISCED 3	ISCED 1	ISCED 2	ISCED 3	ISCED 1	ISCED 2	ISCED 3
Austria	10	–	66	65	–	7	8	–	27	27
Belgium	60	73	73	73	27	27	27	0	0	0
France	20	62	63	63	14	21	21	24	16	16
Portugal	5	82	88	82	0	0	0	18	12	18
Spain	30	65	65	75	13	13	72	22	22	18
United States	10	95	95	95	5	5	5	0	0	0

1. 73 per cent of the decisions considered in this study are taken at school level in the private education sector in Belgium (this figure applies to all three stages of education).

"private education systems"; it would be nearer the mark to speak in terms of individual private schools. However, the fact that most of them are Catholic means that they have a certain degree of homogeneity. In some countries, for example, an implicit structure does exist (non-compulsory, but recommended), which makes for consistency within Catholic education.

Not surprisingly, the United States and Portugal are also the countries where virtually no decisions are taken at the *intermediate levels* in the case of private education. Somewhat more surprisingly, however, this also holds true for ISCED 3 in Spain. Among the other countries, the importance of the intermediate levels can range from 13 per cent (Spain, ISCED 1 and 2) to 27 per cent (Belgium, ISCED 1, 2 and 3). However, the figure is always substantially lower than for public education.

When no decisions are taken at *national level* for public education, the same obviously applies to private education. This is the case in Belgium and the United States. When decisions are taken at this level in the public sector, this is also the case in the private sector, but the importance of this level in the decision-making structure is considerably lower. Going from the public to the private sector, the central government loses slightly over a third of its powers in Spain, almost half in France (ISCED 2 and 3) and about 70 per cent in Portugal, where central government's importance shrinks from half the decisions to about 15 per cent.

The decision-making process in private education in a country is therefore not unrelated to the process in public education. The two have certain features in common: for example, non-intervention by the federal level in the United States and non-intervention by the intermediate levels in Portugal. Where private differs from public education is in the more extensive autonomy of schools, although this autonomy may be greater in some countries (United States, Portugal) than in others (Austria, Belgium, Spain, France).

Conclusions

The first thing to note in both public and private systems is their diversity. No easily identifiable model is common to the majority of countries and the straightforward contrast between centralised and decentralised systems is no longer valid.

On the other hand, of the 14 countries studied, those where there is a dominance either of the school or the local level (LI), or the two together, are in the majority. The origin of this model is twofold: in some countries (Germany, United States) it is a time honoured decision-making model introduced well before considerations of effectiveness assumed the importance they have today in education systems; in others (the Nordic countries) it is a more recent trend in which the concern for effectiveness has undoubtedly played a more important part.

The model that most clearly differs from this is not a centralised system but one where powers are divided more evenly between all of the levels. What this study shows in particular is that schools can have extensive powers even in systems where the national level retains a substantial proportion. This applies to France in the case of ISCED 2 and ISCED 3, to Denmark in the case of ISCED 3, and to Austria, Ireland, New Zealand and Portugal in the case of all three education levels.

It follows from this that, if the intention is to change the decision-making structure of an education system, it is not just one question that has to be considered (should decision-making be moved closer to the "centre" or to the "grassroots"?) but two: how should powers be divided between the school and the intermediate levels, particularly the local level (LI), and how should powers be divided between the national level and the intermediate levels, particularly the regional level (UI)? The response to these questions can favour centralisation in the first case and decentralisation in the second, or vice-versa.

A comparison of the efficiency of decision-making structures could be based on the typologies that have been identified: for example, on the distinction between countries where most decisions are taken by the school or at the local level, and countries where more levels play a significant role. It could also be based on the two above mentioned questions.

The efficiency of a structure may depend not only on the size of the country concerned but also on its history. Because of this history, it may be more "natural" for a particular type of decision to be taken at a particular level, in which case the efficiency objective itself would argue in favour of greater diversity.

The optimum system may well be the one which represents the least imperfect compromise possible between national traditions in education, operational logic and the legitimacy of the country's various administrative and policymaking subdivisions.

Modes of decision-making

When characterising an education system, less importance is usually assigned to the way decisions are taken than to the level at which they are taken. This is perhaps a mistake. Each mode of decision-making has its own inherent virtues and drawbacks. An

49

Table 12. **Modes of decision-making in education systems**[1]

	No. of countries	Autonomy	Consultation	Set framework
Public sector				
ISCED 1	14	53	15	32
ISCED 2	14	52	15	33
ISCED 3	14	50	17	33
Private sector				
ISCED 1	5	70	6	25
ISCED 2	6	66	7	28
ISCED 3	6	68	7	25

1. Out of 100 decisions taken in ISCED 1 public education, 53 per cent are taken completely autonomously by one or other of the three decision-making levels.

autonomous decision is swifter and also less expensive. A decision taken in consultation is certainly slower, but may be safer and more difficult to contest. Those that are taken within a framework set by a higher authority represent an attempt to combine decision-making levels in the most effective way, but the autonomy exercised by the level actually taking the decision varies in relation to the latitude that this framework allows it (Table 12).

The overall picture

In the case of public education the pattern is the same whatever the level: half of the decisions are taken in full autonomy, about 15 per cent in consultation with another level of the system and 30 per cent within a framework set by a higher authority.

In the case of private education the figures are roughly 70 per cent in full autonomy, 10 per cent in consultation and 25 per cent within a set framework. In the private sector, therefore, more decisions are taken autonomously. Decisions taken in consultation are less frequent, as are those taken within a set framework. Nonetheless, those taken within a set framework still represent a sizeable proportion: about one-quarter.

It is interesting to take a look at the distance (in the administrative sense of the number of echelons) between the levels which consult with one another or between the level which sets the framework and that where the decision is taken. For this purpose we shall be confining our attention to public education, noting how many of the decisions that are taken jointly by two levels are taken by two adjoining levels in our four-level structure, *i.e.* the school, the lower and upper intermediate levels, and the highest level.

Not all joint decisions are taken by adjoining levels in the decision-making structure (Table 13). However, the pattern differs substantially depending on whether such decisions are taken in consultation or within a framework set by a higher authority.

Table 13. **Proportion of joint* decisions taken by adjoining levels (Public) (%)**[1]

	Consultation	Set framework
ISCED 1	75	35
ISCED 2	74	32
ISCED 3	58	33

*   A "joint" decision is one involving two levels.
1.   In the case of ISCED 1, 75 per cent of the decisions taken in consultation are taken between two adjoining levels, *i.e.* school and LI, or LI and UI, etc. The column "set framework" covers 14 countries, whereas the column "consultation" covers only 13 since in Austria no decision is taken in this way.

In most countries, *all decisions taken in consultation* are taken between adjoining levels. When such is not the case (*e.g.* Ireland, New Zealand), this is often because what are adjoining levels in these countries (central government, school) are not so in the four-level structure used in this study. In fact, it is fairly difficult to imagine that one level can consult with another that is not adjoining, if it is the adjoining level that has authority as regards the decision concerned.

In the case of *decisions taken within a set framework*, the most common pattern is not that of adjoining levels but that where the school takes a decision within a framework set at the highest level: 43 per cent of the decisions taken within a set framework at ISCED 2 are of this type. The importance in the decision-making structure of a public sector school at ISCED 2 is 38 per cent (Table 5) and we shall be seeing later (Table 16) that 55 per cent of this takes the form of decisions taken within a framework set by a higher authority. The decision-making structure for ISCED 2, therefore, includes about 9 per cent of decisions ($38 \times 0.55 \times 0.43$) that are taken by the school within a framework set at national level, that is to say between 2 and 4 decisions out of the 34 studied.

Thus, what emerges fairly clearly from this is that, whereas the highest level in many education systems takes relatively few decisions, it nonetheless retains a strong influence, over and above the decisions it takes itself, through the number for which it sets the framework. In this respect, it would be interesting to calculate the importance of this level not only by the number of decisions it takes itself but also by the number in which it intervenes.

Country comparison

Public sector, ISCED 2

As with the level at which decisions are taken, the way in which they are taken differs greatly from country to country. In the case of lower secondary education the proportion of decisions taken by one level or another in complete autonomy ranges from 19 per cent (United States) to 70 per cent (Norway), decisions taken in consultation from 0 per cent (Austria) to 44 per cent (United States), and decisions taken within a frame-

51

work set by a higher authority from 16 per cent (Switzerland) to 59 per cent (Finland) (see Table 14).

There are, nevertheless, a number of common characteristics:

– in all countries, except the United States and Finland, decisions taken in complete autonomy are the most numerous;
– in most countries, decisions taken in consultation between several levels are the least numerous;
– a classification similar to the one compiled earlier for the decision-making levels (Table 6) and indicating the main modes of decision-making shows:
  • six countries where autonomous decision-making is the main mode, accounting for about two-thirds or more of all decisions, *i.e.* Austria, Denmark, Norway, New Zealand, Portugal, Switzerland;
  • two countries where consultation accounts for less than 10 per cent of the decision-making structure and where the two other modes together make up 90 per cent or more of this structure, *i.e.* Finland, Sweden;
  • and a further six countries, therefore, where the respective importance of the different modes is less unequal, *i.e.* Germany, Belgium, Spain, United States, Ireland, France. Within this group there are two countries that stand out: Ireland by virtue of the fact that the three modes have virtually the same importance, and the United States because of the frequency of consultation.

What is more, there would not appear to be any link between the respective importance of levels and modes of decision-making. For example, one might have expected that, in countries where schools take many decisions, these would be more

Table 14. **Modes of decision-making in education systems (ISCED 2, Public)** [1]

	Autonomy	Consultation	Set framework
Austria	63		37
Belgium	58	10	33
Denmark	64	18	18
Finland	35	6	59
France	54	13	33
Germany	42	21	37
Ireland	35	33	32
New Zealand	63	4	33
Norway	70	8	22
Portugal	63	8	29
Spain	58	14	28
Sweden	48	6	46
Switzerland	63	21	16
United States	19	44	37

1. Taking all of the decisions considered in the study, in the case of Belgium's ISCED 2 public sector, 58 per cent are taken in complete autonomy by one or other of the four decision-making levels.

52

constrained by consultation or frameworks of various kinds. Although this is true in the case of Ireland, it is the reverse that occurs in New Zealand, *i.e.* not only is autonomy very frequent in New Zealand but its schools take many decisions. We shall be looking at this aspect in more detail in a later section (Section "Modes and levels of decision-making" below) but it is worth noting here and now that there is no simple link between the classification of modes and that of levels of decision-making.

Public sector, ISCED 1 and 3

Annex 3.1 contains the same information as Table 14 but for ISCED 1 and 3. In order to allow for the somewhat unreliable nature of the data on modes, in analysing this information we have applied the principle that two decision-making structures are not considered to be dissimilar unless there is an 8 point difference between them. On this basis, it will be seen that the pattern for modes of decision-making usually remains unchanged when we leave ISCED 2 and look at the two other levels of public education. What is more, the one or two variations that do occur are not indicative of a general trend.

For ISCED 1, in France, autonomy is more frequent and decisions within a set framework less common than in ISCED 2. In Switzerland, consultation loses ground to decisions within a set framework. In Portugal, consultation is more frequent than in ISCED 2.

For ISCED 3, the only notable changes in relation to ISCED 2 are to be seen in Denmark, Norway and Switzerland – in Denmark, autonomy is more frequent at this level, whereas it is less so in the other two countries.

The observations made above for lower secondary education (ISCED 2) can therefore be applied to the entire public sector school system.

Private sector

It will perhaps be recalled that in the private sector, in general, autonomous decisions are more frequent and decisions in consultation less frequent than in the public sector. In fact, at ISCED 2, depending on the country, autonomous decisions account for between 59 and 73 per cent of all decisions and decisions in consultation invariably less than 20 per cent (Table 15).

Three countries are close to the average pattern (Belgium, United States, France) while one, Portugal, stands out by virtue of the complete absence of consultation between different levels of the system.

The pattern for the other stages of education is sometimes different (see Annex 3.4). For example, in France, in the case of private sector primary education (ISCED 1), autonomous decisions are more frequent than in ISCED 2 (80 per cent as against 63 per cent).

In Spain, in the case of upper secondary education (ISCED 3), autonomous decisions are more frequent than in ISCED 2 (77 per cent as against 62 per cent).

Table 15.   **Modes of decision-making in the private and public education systems**
(ISCED 2)

	Autonomy		Consultation		Set framework	
	Private	Public	Private	Public	Private	Public
Austria	70	63	3	0	27	37
Belgium	59	58	17	10	24	32
France	63	54	11	13	26	33
Portugal	73	63	0	8	27	29
Spain	62	58	4	14	34	28
United States	66	19	6	44	27	36

Comparing the public with the private system, the frequency for the different modes of decision-making is substantially the same except in one country, the United States. Whereas the public system in the United States is notable for the frequency of decisions in consultation, these are virtually non-existent in its private education system. Not only do private schools in the United States take almost all of the decisions that concern them (see Table 11) but, in addition, they take over two-thirds of them in complete autonomy, as we shall be seeing later (see Table 18).

Conclusions

In both public and private systems and at all stages of education, most decisions are taken in complete autonomy. This is true as an overall average, true for all private systems and for nine out of the fourteen public systems. What needs to be emphasised, however, is that, in eight out of 14 public systems at ISCED 2, over 40 per cent of the decisions are joint, *i.e.* taken in consultation or within a set framework. In other words, in a majority of the countries studied here the decision-making structure indicates a fairly high degree of integration in terms of the way public sector education is organised. It would, moreover, be interesting to see how this degree of integration compares with that for other organisational systems (*e.g.* health systems, major enterprises).

Identifying these structures prompts the question as to the reasons why countries adopt a particular structure and whether they are happy with it. For example, among the joint decisions, those taken in consultation represent very much a minority except in Ireland, Switzerland and the United States. These three countries have not recently overhauled their formal decision-making structure, nor for that matter has Germany where decisions taken in consultation are relatively numerous. Does this mean that consultation is a good mode of decision-making that satisfies those countries which use it, or that it survives only where it has not been possible to modify the decision-making structure?

Decisions taken within a set framework are often relatively numerous in countries that have changed their decision-making structure (Belgium, Spain, Finland, France,

New Zealand, Sweden), although they are also numerous in some of the longer established structures (United States, Germany).

In the case of this first set of countries, are these decisions whose pattern has been
modified? If so, do they represent a somewhat unsatisfactory compromise invented by
countries as a means of partially decentralising their decision-making process? Or, on the
other hand, is this a modern form of decision-making that makes it possible, thanks to the
power of information systems and an adjustment procedure based on post facto evaluation, to reconcile local autonomy with respect for national guidelines?[8]

All this study can do is to raise such questions, but not to answer them. In order to
identify the changes that have affected these modes of decision-making and, in addition,
to determine the advantages or disadvantages of each of them, longitudinal and/or
bilateral studies would have to be undertaken. It would be necessary to compare not only
the cost of administering an education system depending on which is the predominant
mode of decision-making, but also the appropriateness of these modes, using for this
purpose parameters that are more difficult to measure such as the extent to which
decisions that are taken are applied, the likelihood that they are taken when they need to
be or, on the other hand, their ability to withstand unduly frequent or unwarranted
criticism.

The question of the optimum mode of decision-making must also be seen in conjunction with that of the level of decision-making, despite the fact that, as we saw earlier,
at this stage we can detect no clear link between these two dimensions of the decision-
making process. This is something we shall be trying to establish in the following section.

Modes and levels of decision-making

It is conceivable that two decision-making structures with the same breakdown by
level and mode of decision-making are nevertheless different. All that would be necessary in this case would be, for example, that in one of the structures autonomous
decisions are taken by the school and decisions within a set framework by the regional
level, and that in the other structure the reverse should be the case. It is important
therefore to interrelate the analysis of levels and modes of decision-making.

This we shall be doing in two ways: first, by analysing the aggregate results for all
countries and comparing the frequency of each mode at the different levels; and secondly,
by taking the analysis of the importance of the two main levels, i.e. the school and the
national level, and incorporating therein the concept of the mode of decision-making. As
we saw earlier, the importance of a particular level in the decision-making structure can
be measured in three ways: by the number of decisions it takes, by the number it takes in
complete autonomy and, thirdly, by the number in which it is involved, either because it
takes these decisions itself, is consulted before they are taken or sets the framework in
which they are taken.

We shall be trying to determine to what extent the incorporation of this additional
dimension alters the classifications derived solely on the basis of the level of decision-
making.

Modes and levels in the countries as a whole

One could visualise a model for education systems similar to that for multinational enterprises, with the individual operating units taking many autonomous technical decisions and with the intermediate level (the national subsidiaries) taking decisions within a fairly strict framework set by the international level (the parent company).

In fact, the general trend which emerges for the countries taken as a whole is that, the higher the level within the system, the greater the proportion of autonomous decisions and the smaller the proportion of decisions taken within a set framework (Table 16).

Those who consider autonomous decisions to be the only ones that represent real power are likely to feel that so far we have exaggerated the powers of schools within the *public systems of education*. The fact is that, in the public sector at ISCED 2, over half (55 per cent) of the decisions by schools are taken within a framework set by a higher authority. Decisions within a set framework account for no more than 31 per cent at level LI, 19 per cent at level UI and there are obviously none at national level.

Although the most frequent mode of decision-making in the school is the decision within a set framework, at the other three levels the most frequent is the autonomous decision.

Consultation is not the predominant mode at any level and is of some significance only at the local level (LI): 27 per cent of the decisions taken at this level are taken in consultation, in most cases with the school.

Broadly speaking, it could be said that, in the public sector, schools decide either autonomously or within a set framework, that the local level (LI) is the only one to use all three modes of decision-making to any significant extent and that the level UI takes mainly autonomous decisions and the national level almost exclusively autonomous decisions.

The 52 per cent of decisions taken autonomously in ISCED 2 (Table 12) are split as follows: 14 per cent by the school (given that it takes 38 per cent of decisions and that 38 per cent of these are autonomous, then $38 \times 0.38 = 14$), 13 per cent by level LI, 7 per cent by UI and 18 per cent by the national level. Therefore, looking solely at the autonomous decisions, the national level is the main decision-making level for the 14 countries taken together, while the school takes only between four and seven decisions autonomously out of the 34 studied.

This is also true for ISCED 1 and ISCED 3. The decision-making structures for ISCED 2 and ISCED 3 are very similar. That for ISCED 1 differs somewhat, having a slightly higher proportion at national level of decisions in consultation and a slightly lower proportion at level UI.

In the *private sector* the pattern is virtually identical for all three stages of education. Schools in the private sector take a greater proportion of their decisions in complete autonomy than do those in the public sector. The other levels take so few decisions that it would be unwise to comment on the way these are taken. It can however be said that autonomy is the dominant mode of decision-making at both the regional and national levels, as in the case of the public sector but to an even more marked extent.

Table 16. **Modes and levels of decision-making (public and private sectors, ISCED 1, 2 and 3)**

	No.[1]	Autonomy			Consultation			Set framework		
		ISCED 1	ISCED 2	ISCED 3	ISCED 1	ISCED 2	ISCED 3	ISCED 1	ISCED 2	ISCED 3
Public sector										
School	14	41	38	38	4	7	85	55	55	54
LI	14	44	42	27(8)	27	27	35	29	31	38(8)
UI	7	69	60	60(10)	9	21	20(10)	22	19	20(11)
Central gov.	11	85	93	88(12)	15[2]	7	12(12)	–	–	–
Private sector										
School	5	67	63(6)	66	5	6	7	29	31	28
LI[3]	3	26	–(2)	–(2)	28	39(2)	41(2)	45	61(2)	59(2)
UI[3]	3	73	56	57(4)	11	14	13(4)	16	31	30(4)
Central gov.	3	100	100(4)	100(4)	–	–	–	–	–	–

1. Number of countries in which decisions are taken at this level. Whenever this number differs for a particular stage of education, the actual number of countries concerned is indicated in brackets.
2. With respect to primary education, for the 11 countries where decisions are taken at national level, these are taken in consultation with another level in 15 per cent of cases on average, and autonomously in 85 per cent of cases on average. The percentage figures read across the table for each stage of education and are calculated for the total number of countries in which decisions are taken at the stage concerned. Accordingly, the figures within the same column are not strictly comparable with one another.
3. Only a very small number of decisions are concerned in this case.

We shall be examining hereunder the situation country by country, focusing first on the school level and then on the national level.

Power and the way it is exercised at the school and at the national levels

Schools

In the United States, ISCED 2 *public sector schools* take relatively few decisions (26 per cent, which ranks the country in 12th place out of the 14); they take even fewer in complete autonomy (5 per cent, ranking it 13th out of the 14), but they are consulted on 24 per cent of the decisions taken on their behalf, which means that they are involved in 26 + 24 = 50 per cent of the decisions that concern them, with the result that, on the basis of this particular criterion, the country moves up to third place out of the 14 (Table 17).

What this example shows is not only that, depending on the criterion used, the assessment of a school's "autonomy" can vary, but also that certain education systems are able to make utmost use of the potential variety of modes of decision-making.

Table 17 highlights the major changes that occur in the ranking of countries such as Germany, Belgium and Portugal, depending on which criterion is used. German schools, for example, take only one decision autonomously (3 per cent of the structure) but take

Table 17.   **The power of the schools and the way it is exercised (ISCED 2, Public)** [1]

	Proportion of decisions			
	Taken	Of which, taken in full autonomy	Influenced	Taken or influenced
	(1)	(2)	(3)	(4) = (1) + (3)
Austria	38	14	0	38
Belgium	25	22	5	30
Denmark	41	19	9	50
Finland	40	20	10	50
France	31	13	10	41
Germany	33	3	7	40
Ireland	73	21	5	78
New Zealand	71	38	3	74
Norway	32	14	8	40
Portugal	40	10	2	42
Spain	28	10	7	35
Sweden	48	14	4	52
Switzerland	10	0	10	20
United States	26	5	24	50

1.   In Belgium, in the case of public sector lower secondary schools, out of the 34 decisions concerning them, the schools themselves take 25 per cent (22 per cent in complete autonomy), and are consulted on a further 5 per cent. They are therefore involved in 25 + 5 = 30 per cent of decisions.

more jointly and are consulted on a further two or three decisions, with the result that the figure for their overall involvement in the structure is about average.

Taking the last of these criteria, *i.e.* the decisions in which the school is involved, the ranking of education systems on the basis of the influence of the school itself is as follows:

1. Ireland, New Zealand (> 70 per cent);
2. Denmark, United States, Finland, Sweden (50-52 per cent);
3. Germany, Austria, France, Norway, Portugal (38-42 per cent);
4. Belgium, Spain (30-32 per cent);
5. Switzerland (20 per cent).

Although this is not a hard and fast rule, it would appear that schools in what were previously the more centralised countries (France, Norway, Portugal, Sweden) are nowadays involved in a fairly high proportion of decisions and take a fairly high proportion of these themselves, but take comparatively few decisions autonomously.

By contrast, what could be said to be a general rule is that where the local level (LI) is powerful it will establish a certain degree of consultation with the schools. On average, for the eight countries where this level is strongest (Germany, Belgium, Denmark, United States, Finland, Norway, Sweden, Switzerland) schools are consulted (Table 16, col. 3) in 10 per cent of the decisions that concern them, as against 4 per cent for the six countries where the local level is weaker. There may, however, be one or two exceptions to this rule. For example, it would seem that in Belgium and Sweden the local level rarely consults the schools; they are occasionally consulted in France, despite the fact that no authority is exercised at local level in the case of ISCED 2. Nonetheless, despite these exceptions, there would certainly seem to be a general tendency in this respect.

Another question that arises is whether the classification of these structures varies depending on whether one is considering the proportion of decisions taken in complete autonomy or only those influenced by the school. This is indeed so, although it is impossible to discern any underlying logic in these variations. It might be expected that the greater the number of modes of decision-making incorporated within a criterion, the more the pattern for the various countries would be similar. However, this can scarcely be said to be the case if we compare the decisions in which the school is involved with those that it takes (the standard deviation drops by about 1 point) and, what is more, the variance is very slight in the case of decisions taken in complete autonomy. In other words, given that in most countries (other than New Zealand) public sector schools take relatively few decisions autonomously – less than a quarter of all decisions – the existence of other methods of associating them in the decision-making process does however introduce a substantial degree of variance in the situation of schools in the different countries.

What, therefore, is the most meaningful criterion for assessing the degree of autonomy enjoyed by schools? Unquestionably, the one where the differences between countries are the widest as, for example, with respect to operating costs, performance or some other criterion for evaluating their education system. At this stage in the investigation, however, we can only ask the reader to decide which is more important: for example, the

Table 18. **The power of the schools and the way it is exercised (ISCED 2, Private)**

	Proportion of decisions			
	Taken	Of which, taken in full autonomy	Influenced	Taken or influenced
	(1)	(2)	(3)	(4) = (1) + (3)
Austria	66	41	4	70
Belgium	73	32	0	73
France	63	44	7	70
Portugal	88	60	0	88
Spain	65	40	2	67
United States	95	66	3	98

convergence that was noted in the case of autonomous decisions or the divergence in the case of the decisions in which the school is involved.

Schools in the *private sector* (Table 18) also do not take a very high proportion of decisions autonomously – except in Portugal and the United States – even though they take more than do public sector schools. When the different modes of decision-making are taken into account, it would seem therefore that we need to qualify somewhat the idea put forward earlier that there are individual private sector "schools" rather than private education "systems".

The national level

The importance of the national level can also vary considerably depending on whether or not the decisions that it influences without making them itself are taken into account, *i.e.* where it has to be consulted before they are taken or, more often, where it sets the framework for them (Table 19). When this last criterion is used, the importance of the national level not only becomes much greater – more than doubling on average – but also shows more variation.

The increase in the importance of the national level is particularly substantial in two groups of countries: in Austria, Spain, France and New Zealand roughly 30 per cent of decisions are taken at this level, but it is in fact involved in over 50 per cent; while in Ireland and Finland, although the national level itself takes few decisions (respectively 19 and 13 per cent), it is however involved in a very large number of them (respectively 73 and 61 per cent). In addition, it is worth noting that in the United States 5 per cent of decisions are taken within a framework set at federal level, with the result that Belgium and Switzerland are the only two countries where the national level is involved in none of the decisions.

Lastly, the decisions taken by the national level are more often than not taken autonomously. By definition, it cannot take decisions within a framework set by a higher authority.[9] For the central level therefore, the only other possibility is consultation with a

Table 19. **The power of the national level and the way it is exercised (ISCED 2, Public)**

	Proportion of decisions			
	Taken	Of which, taken in full autonomy	Influenced	Taken or influenced
	(1)	(2)	(3)	(4) = (1) + (3)
Austria	28	28	35	63
Belgium	0	–	0	0
Denmark	15	15	14	29
Finland	13	13	48	61
France	33	30	21	54
Germany	7	7	0	7
Ireland	19	14	54	73
New Zealand	29	25	35	64
Norway	23	23	17	40
Portugal	57	53	33	90
Spain	33[1]	31	24[1]	57
Sweden	4	4	31	35
Switzerland	0	–	–	0
United States	0	–	5	5

1. In Spain, in the case of public sector lower secondary education, 33 per cent of decisions are taken by the national level (31 per cent without any other level being consulted). In addition, the national level influences 24 per cent of the decisions, *i.e.* either it is consulted or it sets the framework for them. It is therefore involved in 33 + 24 = 57 per cent of decisions.

lower level before a decision is taken. This system of consultation is in fact used primarily in those countries where the central level itself takes a fairly substantial number of decisions (Spain, France, New Zealand and Portugal, with Ireland being the only exception to this). In other words, in an education system where many decisions are taken at the national level, more of these are taken in consultation. This tends to disprove the idea that, in centralised systems, the "centre" decides everything, without reference to anyone.

It is therefore clear that education systems to a great extent use modes of decision-making in which several levels participate, and that the importance of these levels is conditioned by the various ways in which this decision-making power is defined.

Levels, modes and fields of decision-making

When a school or any other level takes a decision, in what field is this?

Or, in broader terms, what are the relationships between the level, mode and content of a decision? What "troikas" are the most common? Which are the least common? To what extent do the complex decision-making structures thus revealed seem rational and can they be considered as conducive to efficient operation of the education system?

These are the questions we shall be addressing in this section, looking at the way the different levels take decisions in the various fields, then at the modes of decision-making in each field and, lastly, at all three of these dimensions – modes, levels and fields – taken together.

Levels and fields

The overall picture

a) Public sector

The pattern of decision-making for the "average education system" for public sector lower secondary education (Table 20) has been obtained by allocating the same weight to each country and adding together their replies: decisions taken by the school are primarily in the field of the organisation of instruction; decisions taken by the level immediately above it are primarily in the fields of personnel management and resource allocation; decisions taken at the level above this (UI) involve all four fields.

The decisions taken at national level concern almost exclusively the last three fields, *i.e.* planning and structures, personnel management and resource allocation.

Working on the principle that a level "specialises" in a particular field if this field accounts for over 30 per cent of its contribution to the decision-making structure, the school can therefore be seen as specialising in the organisation of instruction, level LI in personnel management and resource allocation, and the two higher levels (UI and national) in the field of planning and structures. It should however be noted that a

Table 20. **Levels and fields of decision-making in certain OECD countries (ISCED 2, Public)**

Level	No.[1]	OI	PS	PM	RA	Total	Proportion of decisions taken
School[2]	14	52	18	15[3]	16	100	38
Lower intermediate	11	7	16	35	42	100	31
Upper intermediate	8	15	39	23	28	100	12
National	11	7	49	30	14	100	19

1. Number of countries among the 14 where this level is involved in the decision.
2. In the case of ISCED 2 in the public sector, 38 per cent of decisions are taken by the school, half of which (52 per cent) are in the field of the organisation of instruction (OI), 18 per cent in that of planning and structures (PS), 15 per cent in that of personnel management (PM) and 16 per cent in that of resource allocation (RA).
3. The analysis by field uses the same system of weighting as used elsewhere, whereby each field is assigned 25 per cent of the weight for the structure as a whole. The same figure, therefore, represents more primary decisions (items) if it is in the column PM (a field containing 12 items) than it does in the column RA (7 items). Strictly speaking, the figures in the PM column for example should be interpreted as follows: "The decisions taken by schools in this field make up 15 per cent of this level's weight in the decision-making structure. This corresponds to 38 x 0.15 = 5.7 per cent of the decision-making structure, or just under three decisions in the field of personnel management, given the weight of a PM item within the structure, that is to say 25/12 or 2.08 per cent."

Table 21. **Fields of decision-making in public sector schools in 14 OECD countries by ISCED level**

	OI	PS	PM	RA	Proportion of decisions taken
ISCED 1	56	16	15	13	35
ISCED 2	52	18	15	16	38
ISCED 3	50[1]	17	16	17	41

1. For the fourteen countries as a whole, 41 per cent of the decisions taken at ISCED 3 are taken by the school, with 50 per cent of these being in the field of the organisation of instruction.

"specialisation" defined in this way can go hand in hand with low involvement in the field in question, if the level itself is only of minor importance within the structure. For example, level UI takes "on average" only one decision as regards resource allocation, *i.e.* 3 per cent of the decision-making structure and 28 per cent, therefore, of the 12 per cent of decisions taken by this level.

This pattern changes relatively little for the other ISCED levels of education. Hereunder, we shall be looking first at each decision-making level for ISCED 1 and then for ISCED 3 (see data in Annex 3.4).

The decisions taken by primary schools are somewhat more confined to the organisation of instruction (56 per cent compared with 52 per cent at ISCED 2 – see Table 21).

In upper secondary education (ISCED 3) the pattern of decision-making by field for the school is the same as at ISCED 2. By contrast, level UI loses some of its all-round competence, being more involved in management and the allocation of resources (37 per cent of its decisions compared with 28 per cent at ISCED 2) and less in the organisation of instruction (8 per cent of its decisions compared with 15 per cent at ISCED 2).

The decisions taken by the local level (LI) follow substantially the same pattern by field for each of the ISCED stages. At national level, the differences are significant only between ISCED 1 and ISCED 3: the national level specialises somewhat more in personnel management and, since its total contribution to the decision-making structure is the same at all three stages of education, this is at the expense of its involvement in the field of planning and structures.

Nonetheless, the broad pattern for ISCED 2 still holds true: at all three stages of public sector education the school takes mainly decisions regarding the organisation of instruction and the local level mainly decisions regarding management, with the national level concerning itself not only with management but also with the structures and planning of education.

b) Private sector

The school is the only level of any consequence in the decision-making structure of the private sector in the six countries considered. Since, moreover, as was pointed out in

Table 22. **Fields of decision-making in private sector schools in six OECD countries by ISCED level**[1]

	OI	PS	PM	RA
ISCED 1	32	21	26	20
ISCED 2	32	22	26	21
ISCED 3	32	21	26	22

1. Taking the six countries together, 32 per cent of the decisions taken by private sector primary schools concern the field of the organisation of instruction.

Part I, most of the decisions are taken by the school, we shall be confining our analysis to it.

The pattern of decision-making is the same for all three ISCED levels and shows that, in the case of private education, the school takes decisions in all fields (Table 22).

The gap between the public and private sectors is most marked in the field of personnel management: the private sector school takes twice as many decisions as its public sector counterpart (Table 5) and twice as many of these concern personnel management. In other words, the private sector school takes about four times as many personnel management decisions as its public sector counterpart, *i.e.* eight as compared with two.

Country comparison

We shall be confining this comparison of countries to public sector education at ISCED stage 2, beginning with the decisions taken by the *school*.

Taking the average pattern for all the countries concerned, the variations about this mean are substantial. In the case of certain fields – but not all – there is a relationship between the importance of the school in the decision-making structure and its importance in the field in question.

For example, the fewer the powers a school possesses, the more these are confined to the organisation of instruction. Conversely, among the seven countries where the school has the largest degree of autonomy (Austria, Denmark, Finland, Ireland, New Zealand, Portugal, Sweden) there are six where the decisions it takes concern all four fields – the only exception to this being Austria (Table 23). Whenever a school takes decisions in only three of these fields, in four cases out of seven it is personnel management that does not come within its ambit.

On the other hand, in countries where the school is of comparable importance, the patterns of decision-making by field can differ substantially. For example, French schools take very few decisions in the field of planning and structures but, compared with others, a fairly substantial number regarding their resources. The pattern is the reverse in Finland and Denmark, *i.e.* little autonomy as regards resources but more as regards planning and structures.

Table 23. **Fields of decision-making in public sector schools (ISCED 2) by country**

	OI	PS	PM	RA	Proportion of decisions taken
Austria	58	13	–	29	38
Belgium [1]	72	20	–	8	25
Denmark	54	26	11	9	41
Finland	39	36	16	9	40
France	64	–	13	23	31
Germany	67	22	–	11	33
Ireland	30	23	23	24	73
New Zealand	35	15	35	15	71
Norway	56	22	–	22	32
Portugal	48	9	26	17	40
Spain	80	–	8	12	28
Sweden	46	22	17	15	48
Switzerland	100	–	–	–	10
United States	73	19	8	–	26
Total	51	20	14	15	

1. In Belgium, a lower secondary school in the public sector takes 25 per cent of the decisions considered in this survey and of these 72 per cent are in the field of the organisation of instruction.

On the other hand also, a school may take a high proportion of personnel management decisions both in countries where it enjoys a great deal of autonomy (New Zealand, Ireland) and in those where it has a lesser degree of autonomy (Portugal).

To sum up:

- In every case, a high proportion – never less than 30 per cent – of the school's decisions concern the organisation of instruction.
- Generally speaking, the greater a school's autonomy, the broader its powers.
- The most straightforward differentiation is between those countries where the school is involved in all four fields (Denmark, Finland, Ireland, Portugal, Sweden and New Zealand) and those where it is involved in only three (all of the remaining countries except Switzerland where the school is involved only in the organisation of instruction) – the missing field in most cases being personnel management.

It will be remembered that the general tendency in the case of *level LI* is for it to be confined mainly to the management of personnel and resources. Except for Belgium, no country diverges completely from this pattern to the extent that this level never wields a very substantial degree of power in the other two fields (Table 24).

What is true for this level also is that, as its powers increase, so do they widen: in six countries, level LI is involved in all four fields and it is worth noting that these are also

65

Table 24. **Fields of decision-making at the lower intermediate level (LI)**
(ISCED 2, Public)

	OI	PS	PM	RA	Proportion of decisions taken
Austria	–	–	66	34	8
Belgium [1]	8	40	37	16	50
Denmark	7	8	36	49	44
Finland	13	15	27	45	47
Germany	–	17	32	51	42
Ireland	–	11	25	64	8
Norway	16	8	37	40	45
Spain	–	–	32	68	26
Sweden	7	22	34	37	48
Switzerland	–	–	47	53	40
United States	9	24	32	35	71

1. Level LI takes 50 per cent of the decisions in Belgium and 8 per cent of the decisions it takes concern the organisation of instruction within the schools.

the countries where this level has the greatest powers, *i.e.* Belgium, Denmark, United States, Finland, Norway and Sweden.

Nonetheless, nowhere does level LI have substantial powers as regards the organisation of instruction and it is always this field that is missing in those countries where this level wields powers in only three fields. Likewise, it is only in Belgium and the United States that level LI takes more than 20 per cent of its decisions in the field of planning and structures.

Thus, what is noteworthy in this respect is that there is very little diversification of powers. In other words, wherever the local level is stronger than elsewhere it tends to take more management decisions rather than intervening in other fields.

The most significant differentiation, therefore, is between those countries where the intervention of level LI is mainly in the allocation of resources (Denmark, Spain, Finland, Ireland, Germany) and those where this level also intervenes in personnel management (Belgium, United States, Norway, Sweden, Switzerland, Austria).

Level UI intervenes in the decision-making process in only eight countries (Austria, Germany, Spain, France, Belgium, Portugal, Switzerland, United States – and it should be emphasised that in Portugal and the United States it takes only one decision). The wide range of decision-making at this level that was noted in the overall analysis is not really an indication of a general pattern of all-roundness but rather of the fact that, depending on the country concerned, this level can be involved in any of the four fields. It is only in Switzerland that level UI (cantons) intervenes on a broad scale. In Spain, France and Austria it intervenes everywhere else other than in the organisation of instruction. In Belgium, it is the local rather than the regional level that is involved in decisions

Table 25.   **Fields of decision-making at the upper intermediate level (UI)**
(ISCED 2, Public)

	OI	PS	PM	RA	Proportion of decisions taken
Austria	–	14	41	44	26
Belgium	13	–	26	62	25
France	6	30	15	49	36
Germany	17	58	25	–	18
Spain	–	-	26	62	13
Switzerland	31	50	12	7	50

regarding educational planning and structures, and the same is true for Germany in the case of decisions regarding resources (Table 25).

While it can be considered that in most cases there is a rational sharing of powers between the school and the local level – with the school dealing with the organisation of instruction and the local level with management matters – it is not easy to identify any one specific role within the decision-making structure as being that of the regional level. To some extent this is due to the fact that these regional levels may perform two different functions, *i.e.* that of being in effect the highest level in countries where the national level has few or no powers (*e.g.* Belgium and Switzerland) and that of an intermediate level between the local and national levels (*e.g.* France).

Taking the countries as a whole, the *national level* intervenes little in the organisation of instruction but to a significant degree in the other three fields. The pattern, however, varies widely from country to country (Table 26), but it is true in every case that the national level intervenes very little in the field of the organisation of instruction (*e.g.* one decision in Finland) or not at all.

One would expect that the national level would intervene primarily in the field of educational planning and structures, given that this field is covered to a lesser extent by the other three levels. However, this is the case in only six countries (Austria, Denmark, Spain, Norway, Portugal, Sweden) out of the 11 where the national level is involved in decision-making.[10] The main field of decision-making at national level can also be either resource allocation (New Zealand) or personnel management (France, Finland, Germany).

As in the case of the other levels it is apparent that, the greater the powers of the national level, the more wide-ranging these are. Where the national level takes less than 10 per cent of the decisions, it takes these in only one field (Germany, Sweden). Where it takes between 10 and 29 per cent, these are divided between two or three fields; it is only when the national level takes more than 30 per cent that these decisions cover all four fields. What is surprising, however, are the exceptions to this general and seemingly logical rule, which are Ireland (where 19 per cent of decisions are split between the four fields) and France. In the case of France, although the national level takes 33 per cent of

Table 26. **Fields of decision-making at the national level (ISCED 2, Public)**

	OI	PS	PM	RA	Proportion of decisions taken
Austria	11	57	32	–	28
Denmark [1]	–	70	30		15
Finland	24	28	48	–	13
France	10	44	47	–	33
Germany	–	–	100	–	7
Ireland	16	37	32	14	19
New Zealand	–	50	–	50	29
Norway	–	63	37	–	23
Portugal	6	37	25	32	57
Spain	10	63	22	6	33
Sweden	–	100	–	–	4

1. The national level takes 15 per cent of the decisions in Denmark, 30 per cent of which concern personnel management, *i.e.* 4.5 per cent of the decision-making structure. It therefore takes two decisions, given that a personnel management decision represents 2.1 per cent of the total structure.

the decisions, it takes none concerning the allocation and use of resources by the schools: this responsibility is split between the school and the regional level.

By way of conclusion with regard to this cross-tabulation of fields and levels of decision-making, what we can now do is to expand the information contained in the classification of countries by main decision-making levels set out in Table 7.

   a) Where the school takes more than three-quarters of the decisions (Ireland, New Zealand), these naturally concern all four fields, with the national level taking most of the remaining decisions either, once again, in all four fields (Ireland) or with respect to educational structures and resources (New Zealand).

   b) Where the local level (LI) takes more than half of the decisions (Belgium, United States), these concern the organisation of instruction to only a slight extent and to a far greater degree the other three fields. In this case, the school takes about one-quarter of the decisions, 70 per cent of which concern the organisation of instruction and 20 per cent planning and structures. In terms of the decision-making structure, therefore, these two countries' systems of public education appear to be very similar, despite the difference of scale and the much greater importance of private education in Belgium.

   c) In the case of those education systems where the school and level LI together take over 75 per cent of the decisions (Germany, Denmark, Finland, Norway, Sweden), Germany nonetheless differs from the Nordic countries: what we see in Germany is a school whose decisions are virtually confined to the organisation of instruction and curricula (structures), a level LI which does not get involved in the organisation of instruction, the *Länder* (UI) which intervene in three fields – including, to a slight extent, in the organisation of instruction – and a national level that plays very little part, at least as far as the decisions analysed herein are concerned.

In the Nordic countries, level LI intervenes in all four fields and it can be the case that the school takes one or two decisions with regard to personnel management (Denmark, Finland, Sweden) and that the national level plays a significant role in two fields (Norway and, to a lesser extent, Denmark).

d) Those countries where the locus of decision-making is more evenly divided between the levels clearly resemble one another as regards the way the various levels intervene in the different fields. However, this resemblance needs to be qualified in the case of Spain, given that the present configuration of its education system is the result of the juxtaposition of two systems, one of which is intended in due course to replace the other.

In short, consideration of the fields increases rather than decreases the impression of diversity conveyed by the pattern of decision-making in these education systems. There are, however, a number of highly logical constants – such as the importance of the school as regards the organisation of instruction and of the local level as regards management functions, the relationship between the importance and diversification of certain levels – which indicate that this diversity does not betoken a lack of concern that the system should at least be functional if not efficient. What is more, consideration of the fields tends to bear out the classification that was suggested solely on the basis of the decision-making levels (Table 6) to the extent that, in countries belonging to a particular group within this classification, the way the various levels intervene in the different fields is also similar in many cases.

Table 27. **Modes and fields of decision-making (Public)**

Decisions	No.	OI	PS	PM	RA	Proportion of decisions taken
ISCED 1						
autonomy	14	24	24	26	26	53
consultation	13	11	26	29	35	15
set framework	14	33	26	22	19	32
ISCED 2						
autonomy[1]	14	24	25	25	26	52
consultation	13	14	19	32	36	15
set framework	14	32	28	22	18	33
ISCED 3						
autonomy	14	25	24	26	25	50
consultation	13	10	23	29	38	17
set framework	14	33	28	21	18	33

1. Decisions taken autonomously account for 52 per cent of the decision-making structure in lower secondary education (ISCED 2). They are divided between the four fields in such a way that the proportion of decisions (items) taken in each of them is identical.

Modes and fields

As we have seen, there is a certain inherent logic in the relationships that have been noted between levels and fields (the fact that the school is concerned mainly with the organisation of instruction, the local level with the management of personnel and resources, etc.), or between levels and modes (the frequency of decisions taken autonomously by the school within a set framework, by the higher levels within the structure, etc). It is less easy to discern any logical relationship between modes and fields of decision-making. One would expect to find more frequent consultation in the case of decisions in the field of personnel management but, as was noted earlier, this type of consultation, *i.e.* between employer and unions at the same level within the system, does not come within the scope of this study. Apart from this example, it is difficult to imagine a theory which, for instance, calling above all for rapid decision-making in a particular field, would advocate that most decisions should be autonomous. What we shall be doing here is to look therefore at the frequency of linkages between modes and fields in order to identify one or two constants. The analysis in this case will be confined to public sector education, given that the private sector would be less meaningful in this respect due to the overwhelming predominance of autonomous decisions.

Overall analysis

In lower secondary education (ISCED 2), the autonomous decisions taken by one or other level within the system are divided almost completely evenly between the four fields.

By contrast, decisions taken in consultation more often concern personnel management and resource allocation. It will be remembered that the local level (LI), which in most cases has responsibility in these two fields, is also the level that makes most frequent (or rather, least infrequent) use of consultation. Does LI practice consultation because consultation is associated with these fields for which it happens to be responsible? Or is consultation associated with these fields because LI has responsibility for them and because LI is an appropriate level for consultative decision-making? These are the sort of questions that this study can raise, but obviously not answer. Nonetheless, they are extremely relevant. In the second case, the example of the others would tend to encourage a country that wanted to strengthen its local level (LI) to promote at the same time a consultative form of decision-making at this level. In the first case, no such incentive would exist unless it was intended to extend the authority of LI in the two fields in question (PM and RA) (Table 27).

Decisions taken within a framework set by another level[11] are more frequent in the case of the organisation of instruction by virtue of the fact that this mode of decision-making is more common at school level than it is at the other levels, and the fact that the school is usually responsible for the organisation of instruction.

The pattern for ISCED 1 and 3 is virtually identical to that for ISCED 2, which is the reason why we shall be considering only ISCED 2 in the following analysis by country.

There is, however, a slight variation that occurs in both ISCED 1 and ISCED 3: decisions taken in consultation are more evenly divided between the three fields other than the organisation of instruction, and somewhat less concentrated on the management of personnel and resources than in ISCED 2.

Analysis by country (ISCED 2, Public)

Looking at the data by country (Table 28) it becomes apparent that the balance between fields as regards the frequency of *autonomous decisions* is the result of aggregating what are very different situations.

Autonomous decisions are more common in resource allocation than in the other fields in the case of Belgium, Denmark, Norway, New Zealand, Sweden and Switzerland. They are more common in the organisation of instruction than in the other fields in the case of Belgium, the United States, Finland, France and Ireland. They are more common in personnel management in the case of Germany, Spain and the United States.

It is clearly in planning and structures that the pattern for the countries is the most similar in this respect, and in resource allocation that it is the least similar.

The pattern also differs from one country to another in the case of *decisions taken in consultation*, notwithstanding the fact that decisions of this kind are fewer in number. Leaving aside those countries where 10 per cent or less of the decisions are taken in consultation, there is a shift away from the overall pattern (Table 28, "Total" line) and more towards planning and structures in the case of Germany, towards the organisation of

Table 28.   **Modes and fields of decision-making in 14 education systems (ISCED 2, Public)**

	Autonomy					Consultation				
	OI	PS	PM	RA	Total	OI	PS	PM	RA	Total
Austria	15	26	31	28	63	–	–	–	–	–
Belgium	38	11	17	34	58	20	–	65	15	10
Denmark	24	28	14	34	64	17	–	63	20	18
Finland	45	31	24	–	35	–	–	100	–	6
France	33	33	23	11	54	–	27	46	27	13
Germany[1]	15	25	35	25	42	–	34	32	34	21
Ireland	45	21	27	8	35	10	11	12	67	33
New Zealand	30	17	20	34	63	–	100	–	–	4
Norway	15	26	24	36	70	–	–	100	–	8
Portugal	20	28	23	29	63	57	43	–	–	8
Spain	16	33	33	19	58	22	29	–	50	14
Sweden	26	15	22	37	48	–	–	100	–	6
Switzerland	5	32	30	34	63	59	24	–	17	21
United States	38	25	37	–	19	–	22	22	56	44
Total	24	25	25	26	52	14	19	32	36	15

1.   In Germany, 42 per cent of the decisions taken in ISCED 2 public sector education are taken in full autonomy by one or other of the levels in the decision-making structure; 35 per cent of these 42 per cent (*i.e.* 15 per cent of the 34 decisions studied) are decisions regarding personnel management.

instruction in the case of Switzerland, towards personnel management in the case of Denmark and France, and towards resource allocation in the case of Spain, the United States and Ireland.

A similar degree of diversity is apparent as regards *decisions taken within a framework set by another level*. It is therefore likely that the logic determining the mode of decision-making takes little account of the field to which a decision belongs. The picture might well be different if we had used another classification of decision-making modes, this one being probably too much centred on the administrative levels within an education system.

Modes, levels and fields

How do the classifications that emerge from the analysis of decision-making levels fit in with those deriving from the analysis of decision-making modes? Does this make it possible to measure the proximity of the education systems more accurately and more comprehensively than we have been able to do so far? Do some decisions more than others separate the countries into different groups? If so, is this because they are taken at a given level, in a given way, or both?

These are questions that the foregoing analyses raise but do not answer. To try to answer them, two classical forms of data analysis have been used: factor analysis of correspondence and subsequently a hierarchical classification. Both of these were confined solely to ISCED 2, Public.

Factor analysis of correspondence is a statistical method that is particularly useful when there is a considerable amount of information to be processed.

It highlights those variables that differentiate most sharply the "individuals" (in this case, the decision-making processes within the various countries) and the relationships that exist between these variables (for example, that within a particular country where the schools themselves hire the teaching staff, they also, as a general rule, take the decisions affecting these teachers' careers, but not necessarily their salary scales: see below). There is no need to introduce prior assumptions when conducting such an analysis.

In this particular analysis, the 14 "individuals" are each described by 238 "variables" representing the different possible types of response to the 34 "items" in the questionnaire: four levels of decision-making (school, LI, UI, central government); three modes of decision-making (A, B, C).[12] For example, France's reply regarding the selection of school books [P4, decided autonomously (A) by the school (E)] will be denoted by assigning the value of 1 to P4A and P4E, and 0 to the other possible modes of decision-making (P4B, P4C, P4LI, P4UI, P4central government). In this way we can proceed from a qualitative assessment to a quantified definition of the decision-making process. In fact, the analysis covers 214 "variables", the remaining 24 having been eliminated because their occurrence was either nil or equal to the number of countries. For example, in all 14 countries the pupils' school careers (P2) are never decided at the lower intermediate level or at the national level. The two "variables" P2LI and P2central government were therefore omitted from the analysis. In addition, since the methods of evaluating pupils' normal work (P8) are invariably decided by the school, this variable was also left out.

This analysis helps us to establish a set of factors that can be represented as axes on a graph. These axes consist of a centre of gravity and two extremities around which are clustered the individuals (and the variables) that are most akin to one another and differ the most from the other extremity.

In this case, the first four "axes" explain 47 per cent of the total variance in the replies, that is to say the information represented by the interrelationships between the 68 (34 × 2) elements describing each of the 14 countries.

There are two major factors that explain the differences between the decision-making structures of the education systems. The first of these contrasts extensive involvement of the school in the field of personnel management (coupled with a number of interventions on the part of the national level with regard to resources and credentialling) with the existence of powers at the upper intermediate level in a field where it rarely has such authority, *i.e.* the organisation of instruction and the planning of the educational process. This factor explains 16 per cent of the variance between the countries. In particular, it highlights the contrast between Ireland and New Zealand on the one hand and Switzerland on the other.

The second factor, which explains 15 per cent of the variance, contrasts a powerful local level (LI), intervening in both personnel management and planning, coupled with extensive use of consultation as regards the use and allocation of resources and personnel management (the United States being the country closest to this extremity) with the existence of extensive powers at the national level particularly in the field of personnel management (France and Portugal being the countries closest to this extremity).

These two factors define a space (Figure 1) where what is particularly noticeable is not only the contrast between the countries just mentioned, but also the relative proximity first of the Nordic countries, secondly of Germany and Belgium, and thirdly of Spain and Austria. What is also noticeable on the first axis is the distance separating what are three somewhat unique systems of education (Ireland, New Zealand, Switzerland) with the remaining countries being very close to one another, whereas on the second axis the countries are more evenly spread. The local versus national factor, therefore, structures all of the 14 countries to quite a considerable extent, despite the fact that there is no, or no longer, the contrast between systems where everything is decided by one or the other level.

In addition, it should be noted that the structuring effect is the importance of the local level (LI) versus that of the national level, and not that of the school versus the national level.

The way these two axes are defined is as follows.

Axis 1, at the Ireland and New Zealand end:

– the school decides salary levels for non-teaching staff within a set framework (R3-3);

Figure 1a. **The distinctive features of the 14 decision-making structures**

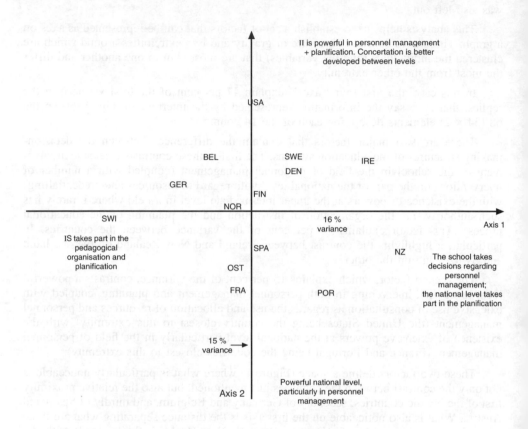

II is powerful in personnel management + planification. Concertation is better developed between levels

USA

BEL   SWE   IRE
DEN
GER
FIN
NOR

SWI   16 % variance   Axis 1

IS takes part in the pedagogical organisation and planification

SPA   NZ

OST   The school takes decisions regarding personnel management; the national level takes part in the planification

FRA   POR

15 % variance

Axis 2   Powerful national level, particularly in personnel management

Source: D. Meuret.

- the school hires both teaching staff (R1-2) and non-teaching staff (R1-3), determines the career of the school principal, the teaching and the non-teaching staff (R1-4?), and plans its own courses on the basis of the subject matters taught (S3);
- the national level, for its part, allocates resources for teaching staff (F1-1) and is responsible for credentialling.

Axis 1, at the Switzerland end:[13]

UI, in consultation with the school, decides what schoolbooks are used (P4) and pupils' school careers (P2). It also decides the length of schooling time (P3), the way

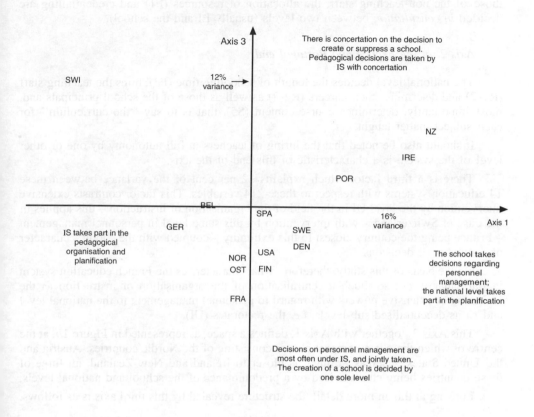

Source: D. Meuret.

resources earmarked for the school's operating expenditure should be used (F2-3), the range of subject matters taught by the school (S4) and the way the courses it provides should be designed.

Axis 2, at the United States end:

The local level (LI) plans the courses on the basis of subject matters (S3) and decides the range of courses offered by each school within its jurisdiction (S4). It sets salary levels (R3) for teachers and the school principal, and decides on how resources allocated for operating expenditure should be used (F2-3).

In addition, the hiring of teachers, their duties and conditions of service as well as those of the non-teaching staff, the allocation of resources (F1) and credentialling are decided *in consultation* between two levels (usually LI and the school).

Axis 2, at the France and Portugal end:

The national level decides the length of schooling time (P3), hires the teaching staff (R1-2) and determines their careers (R4-2) as well as those of the school principals and, most importantly, determines course content (S5), that is to say "the curriculum" for each subject matter taught.

It should also be noted that the hiring of teachers in full autonomy by one or other level of the system is a characteristic of this end of the axis.

There is a third factor which explains 12 per cent of the variance between these 14 education systems with respect to these 214 variables. This factor contrasts extensive intervention by the level UI in the field of the organisation of instruction – this applies in the case of Switzerland – with intervention by this same level in personnel management – France being the country closest to this extremity – coupled with the "joint" character of a number of decisions.

On the basis of this study, therefore, what characterises the French education system in particular is not so much a centralisation of the organisation of instruction as the assigning of extensive powers with regard to personnel management to the national level and to its decentralised sub-levels, *i.e.* the rectorates (UI).

This Axis 3, together with Axis 1, defines a space, as represented in Figure 1*b*, at the centre of which there is a compact cluster consisting of the Nordic countries, Austria and the United States, whereas Portugal is closer to Ireland and New Zealand, all three of these countries being characterised by a predominance of the school and national levels.

Looking at this in more detail, the structure revealed by this third axis is as follows.

At the Switzerland end:

UI decides, *in consultation*, pupils' school careers (P2), the school books used (P4) and the methods of grouping pupils. It also decides the range of subject matters taught and the way funds earmarked for operating expenditures should be used.

In addition, the decision to create or close a school (S1) is taken in consultation whereas ...

at the France end of the axis:

... this decision is taken *autonomously*. What is more, at this end of the axis UI decides on the hiring of non-teaching staff and their careers. However, decisions regarding the careers of both non-teaching and teaching staff, as well as school principals, are taken *in consultation* (R4). Lastly, terms and conditions of service for school principals are defined at the national level.

In Figure 1a and b the countries are compared within the space determined by the main factors of disparity. Figure 2 sets out a classification that was obtained by using as much as possible of the information that was gathered.[14]

Beginning by the countries that are closest to one another, there are first of all Denmark and Sweden, which have often appeared together with one another in the classifications, and then Germany and Norway. In the case of Germany and Norway, the school and LI have the same importance but they differ in that in Germany the national level and LI share the remaining powers which, in Norway, are wielded solely by the national level. However, the proximities established here take account of the nature and not just the number of decisions taken by a particular level. For instance, Denmark and Sweden can be seen to be the two countries where, more than in any other pair of countries, the same decisions are taken at the same level and in the same manner.

Figure 2. **Countries represented according to the proximity of their education system's decision structure (hierarchical classification)**

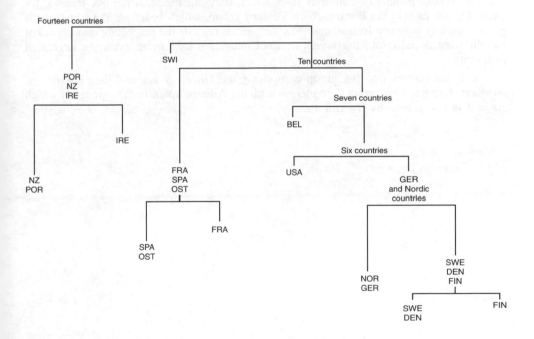

Education systems have stronger affinities when moving down the chart.
Source: D. Meuret.

77

These are followed by the group comprising Denmark, Finland and Sweden, countries which are characterised among other things by the fact that a substantial proportion of the powers is assigned to the school and the local level.

Next comes the Austria/Spain pairing, two countries where all four levels within the system exercise powers, and which are joined by France to form a group of countries where the powers are divided evenly between the school, the two intermediate levels taken together and the national level – a group which has frequently been singled out during the course of this study, but in connection with which it should be borne in mind that Spain's place within it is due to the juxtaposition of two systems, one predominantly national and the other predominantly local in character.

Germany, Norway and the three other Nordic countries form a group whose homogeneity is similar to that of the group comprising Austria, Spain and France.

They are joined by the United States (thus forming a group of countries where what may be a relevant factor is that they all have a protestant culture) at a degree of proximity similar to that for the New Zealand/Portugal pairing, a particular feature of which is the very limited involvement of the intermediate levels.

It is at this point that what might be called "proximities" cease. These are followed by countries that are more individual in character, which progressively become incorporated into those groups of countries from which they are the least remote. Ireland, for example, moves into the Portugal/New Zealand group, which bears out the fact that the great similarity between Ireland and New Zealand as regards the respective importance of the different decision-making levels was not indicative of a more extensive degree of proximity.

Belgium moves into the group comprising the United States and the countries of Northern Europe. This group then merges with the Austria/Spain/France group, at which stage it is also joined by Switzerland.

Conclusions

It goes without saying that the sample of 14 countries used in this study is not representative either of the OECD Member countries and, still less, of all countries throughout the world. The sample is primarily a European one, since only two out of the 14 countries are outside of this area (*i.e.* the United States and New Zealand). A number of countries whose decision-making process is often taken as a reference, such as Japan or the United Kingdom, are not included.

The description of the "average education system" obtained by aggregating the replies from these 14 countries is therefore representative only of this particular set of countries. Nonetheless, it was felt that this was not entirely valueless, if only to establish a benchmark against which each individual country could then be compared.

What therefore are the salient features of this "average education system"?

This can be described by referring to only one stage of education, namely ISCED 2. Although in most countries there are certainly differences between the way the three stages of public sector education are organised, it is apparent that:

- These differences are mainly between ISCED 3 and the stages ISCED 1 and 2 which comprise compulsory education.
- they are, in any case, limited: the school at ISCED 3 has slightly more autonomy than its counterpart at ISCED 1, but takes only two or three more decisions than the latter.

The pattern of decision-making in private sector education is virtually the same at all three stages of education.

At ISCED 2 Public the *school* takes 38 per cent of the decisions affecting its functioning, over half of them within a framework set at a higher level. It takes only between four and seven decisions in full autonomy, of which 50 per cent concern the organisation of instruction and 20 per cent educational planning and structures. Other than in the United States, the school is consulted relatively rarely by the higher levels before they take a decision, with the result that its importance in the decision-making process is scarcely much more than what it derives from the decisions it takes on its own.

The private school at ISCED level 2, whether grant-maintained or not, has far greater autonomy and all-around competence, at least in terms of the average for the six countries studied. Out of 100 decisions affecting its functioning it takes 75, of which

47 in full autonomy. Only 32 per cent of the decisions it takes concern the organisation of instruction, with the remainder being fairly evenly divided between the three other fields. The autonomy enjoyed by private schools does not amount to complete independence, firstly because half of the decisions that affect the schools are not taken by them in full autonomy and, secondly, because they may well be subject to non-official standardising mechanisms. What this does show however, as indeed does the existence of public sector systems where the school takes many decisions (*e.g.* New Zealand, Europe's Nordic countries), is that it is possible to assign more powers to schools than those possessed at present by public sector schools in most of the countries. Whether that would be desirable as regards the effectiveness or the equity of the education systems is, however, a question which this study is unable to answer.

The extensive autonomy of private sector schools makes it less necessary, and indeed more tricky, to analyse the part played by the other decision-making levels in private education. In the public system, the *local level (LI)* takes just under one-third of the decisions, 43 per cent of which in full autonomy and 27 per cent in consultation. The relative frequency of these consultative decisions is, moreover, what distinguishes the local level from the others. It is involved primarily in the management of personnel and resources. In those countries where it is the predominant level, its functions are more diversified, but less perhaps than might be expected: in such countries, it exercises greater authority primarily in the two management fields.

The *upper intermediate level (UI)* takes few decisions, 12 per cent on average, 60 per cent of which are in full autonomy. Depending on the country concerned, its powers can extend to any of the four fields. This level, which does not exist in all of the countries, can play two different roles: either that of the highest level within the system in cases where the national level has no powers in the field of education (Belgium, United States, Switzerland), or that of the intermediate level to which central government entrusts the management of part of the system, as in the case of Austria and France where its powers concern primarily personnel management and the allocation of resources.

The *national level* takes 19 per cent of the decisions, virtually all in full autonomy since it consults to a very limited extent with the lower levels. Moreover, taking into account the decisions that it influences, either by setting the framework for them or because it has to be consulted before they are taken, it can be said to be involved in about 40 per cent of the decisions. Its decisions concern the three fields other than the organisation of instruction and it sets the framework for a good proportion of the decisions taken by the school in this latter field. It should also be borne in mind that the national level takes a number of broad decisions that are not covered in this study. Its influence on the functioning of schools is therefore far from negligible.

Around this average pattern there is considerable diversity, although this diversity does seem to obey certain rules.

There is one decision-making structure that is more common than any other: that where the vast majority of the powers are exercised by the school or by the *local level (LI)*, or by the two between them. However, this type of structure varies, being conditioned by historical factors, specific aims and circumstances.

What is more, the structure which differs most from this is that where the powers are divided equally between the different levels. There is no, or no longer, what could be called a "centralised" public education system, if by this is meant, for example, a system where the national level takes more than half of the decisions and where the school takes less than a third.

In some countries (Austria, Spain, France, New Zealand, Portugal) the national level has more powers than in others but, with the exception of Portugal, these powers extend to less than 35 per cent of the decisions. Moreover, these countries are not ones where the schools are the most lacking in autonomy.

In fact, those countries where the intermediate levels – particularly the local level (LI) – are powerful tend to allow their schools rather less autonomy than the others, although some of the Nordic countries have recently set up systems in which both the schools and the local level are powerful.

However, it is important to take into account the modes of decision-making. Consultation and decisions taken within a set framework are by no means marginal forms of decision-making, including, in the case of the latter, within the private sector. They exist in most of the countries and far outnumber the other modes in Finland and Sweden. The local (LI) and national levels, in those countries where they are powerful, make great use of consultation. Moreover and more particularly, the "ranking" of the countries can change considerably depending on whether the importance of a decision-making level is measured in terms of the decisions it takes in full autonomy, those it takes irrespective of the mode or those in which it is involved. This is the case notably in Germany and the United States with regard to the importance of the school, and in Ireland and New Zealand with regard to the importance of the national level.

Some of the aspects of this diversity would seem to be logical. It is apparent for example that, the fewer decisions the school takes, the more these are confined to the field of the organisation of instruction; the more it takes, then the more these concern all four fields. Whether it does or does not take personnel management decisions is, moreover, one of the most effective criteria in establishing a distinction between the countries.

It is also apparent that, on average, consultative decisions are more common in the fields of personnel and resource management than in the other two fields. However, it is impossible even to guess why this is so to a far greater extent in some countries than in others. By and large, the logic determining the mode of decision-making seems to take little account of the field in which this decision-making occurs.

It is tempting to conclude from all this that, in some countries at least – probably the majority – the decision-making structure, fashioned perhaps by the whims of history, is not the best either in terms of effectiveness or in terms of equity. In our view such a conclusion, although perhaps correct, is nonetheless premature, given that there is no proof that a structure which works well in one country will do so in another or, indeed, that historical factors may not also have a bearing on the suitability of a particular structure. A fact that should be borne in mind in this respect is that those countries whose 9 and 13 year-old pupils demonstrated the highest reading ability – Finland, France and Switzerland – have very different systems of decision-making.[15]

Compiling classifications using statistical techniques that reduce to a minimum the amount of information that is "lost", allows to highlight a number of aspects. Firstly, the distinction between systems assigning more importance to the local level (LI) and those assigning more importance to the national level is still a meaningful one, more meaningful in fact than that which opposes the school and the national level.

This opposition would seem to depend mainly on the way powers as regards personnel management are assigned.

Secondly, there is one other fundamental distinction which is that between countries which divide powers between the national level and the school and those where the intermediate levels play an important role.

Three groups of countries emerge, around which the others (Belgium, Ireland, Switzerland) occupy a more individual position. In Portugal and in New Zealand most of the powers are divided between the school and the national level. Austria, Spain and France resemble one another primarily by virtue of the relatively evenly balanced importance of the three levels within their systems. Germany, the United States and the Nordic countries resemble one another on account of, among other things, the importance of the local level (school and/or LI).

Notes

1. An earlier version of this method had previously been applied within the context of a Franco-Quebec co-operation project. See: CIEP (1990).

2. Conflicts of this kind, which to a certain extent are inevitable, can be resolved by applying a weighting factor to these decisions or by attributing it to more than one decision-making mode. Greater weight can be assigned to an item that incorporates a number of basic decisions. One part of the decision can also be considered to be the framework in which the other part is taken. In France, for example, teachers' conditions of service are determined at the national level. At ISCED level 1 the convenience of the timetable and the pleasantness or unpleasantness of the class do not differ within a particular school. In this case, the answer given was that R2-2 was determined at the national level. On the other hand, at ISCED 2 a teacher's conditions of service are governed primarily by his timetable, which is determined by the school principal. In this case, the answer given was that R2-2 was determined at the level of the school but within a framework set by a higher authority (see Section ''Modes of decision-making'').

3. ''Classe'', meaning ''a group of pupils following education together'', was translated as ''grade'', that is to say another meaning of the word ''classe''.

4. One of the reasons why the powers historically concentrated in Madrid are being devolved to the *comunidades autonomas* is to ''encourage democratic decision-making'' (OECD, 1986, p. 3).

5. *Ibid*. In this argument, decentralisation is seen as a barrier against the standardisation of the world, although there are others who consider that the world is diversifying rather than standardising, in which case decentralisation makes it easier to adapt to this diversification. The equivalent arguments in favour of centralisation would be that the management and administration of education systems should not be fragmented at a time when the economy and information technologies are assuming a worldwide dimension, or, conversely, that in a world where there is a growing tendency towards divisions and a revival of particularisms, this needs to be countered by the barrier of centralised systems.

6. It should be borne in mind that countries were instructed not to fill in the questionnaires for private education unless this accounted for more than 5 per cent of enrolment. It should also be borne in mind that the definition of ''private education'' differs from one country to another, particularly in terms of whether it is subsidised by central government (as in France and Spain), funded by central government on an equal footing with public education (Belgium, Netherlands) or receives no official financial assistance whatsoever (as in the United States).

7. It should be remembered that, in the case of this commentary, only differences of more than 4 percentage points between countries for a particular parameter are considered as significant.

8. However, let it be said at this point that it is not always easy to differentiate between an autonomous decision and one taken within a set framework and that, depending on countries, levels and stages of education, slight differences of appreciation are probably inevitable.

9. In fact, it is conceivable that a "higher" level is called upon to select one out of a number of possible solutions submitted to it by a "lower" level. However, this is a procedure that is apparently not used in the 14 education systems studied here, at least in the case of ISCED 1, 2 and 3.

10. These decisions concern educational structures (items S3 and S7) rather than educational planning (items S1 and S2) – it would perhaps be worthwhile to refine the analysis by differentiating these two dimensions to a greater extent.

11. Generally, this means decisions taken within a framework set by a higher level. However, in the case where a school would ask LI to select a teacher from among three candidates it has shortlisted, then the decision is taken within a framework set by a lower level.

12. $(34 \times 4) + (34 \times 3) = 238$.

13. Note that the parameters characterising this axis do not correspond exactly to the Swiss system, but to a situation to which Switzerland is closer than the other countries. This is of course also true for the other axes and for the countries which serve as their markers.

14. The method used is an ascending hierarchical classification. The results are presented in the form of a dendrogram, the base of which is the 14 education systems. First of all, the two closest systems are grouped together and then this procedure is repeated by calculating the proximities between this first group and all the remaining systems. Thus, step by step, the summit of the tree is reached.

15. IEA Reading Literacy Study, *cf. Que sait-on sur les connaissances des élèves?*, Dossier Education et Formation, No. 17, DEP, ministère de l'Éducation nationale, 1992, Paris.

Bibliography

BELLAT, D.M. and VAN ZANTEN, A. (1992), *Sociologie de l'école*, Armand Colin, Paris.

CIEP (1990), "La performance et l'efficacité des établissements d'enseignement secondaire", Dossiers No. 20, Centre pour la coopération franco-québécoise, Paris, December.

DEROUET, J.L. (1987), "Approches ethnographiques en sociologie de l'éducation", in *Revue française de pédagogie*, No. 78.

EURYDICE EUROPEAN UNIT (1991), "The Division of Powers within the Education Field", published for the EEC, February.

GARNIER, M., HAGE, J. and FULLER B. (1989), "The Strong State, Social Class and Controlled School Expansion in France, 1881-1975", in *American Journal of Sociology*, Vol. 95, No. 2.

HOLMES, B. (1979), *International Guide to Education Systems*, UNESCO, Geneva.

KODRON, C. and HUCK, W. (1993), "Le temps et l'école en ex-RFA", in *Vers l'éducation nouvelle*, No. 459, Paris.

LECLERCQ, J.M. and RAULT, C. (1992), *Quelle formation pour les 16-19 ans d'ici et d'ailleurs?*, L'Harmattan, Paris.

OECD (1984), *Reviews of National Policies for Education: Portugal*, Paris.

OECD (1986), *Reviews of National Policies for Education: Spain*, Paris.

OECD (1990a), *Reviews of National Policies for Education: Norway*, Paris.

OECD (1990b), *Curriculum Reform: An Overview of Trends,* Paris.

OECD (1991a), *Reviews of National Policies for Education: Ireland*, Paris.

OECD (1991b), *Reviews of National Policies for Education: Switzerland*, Paris.

OECD (1992), *Education at a Glance/Regards sur l'éducation,* Paris.

OECD (1993), *Education at a Glance/Regards sur l'éducation*, Paris.

OECD (1994), *School: A Matter of Choice*, Paris.

OECD (1995), *Education at a Glance*, Paris.

SCHEERENS, J. (1992), *Effective Schooling, Research, Theory and Practice,* Cassel, London.

Annex 1

Number of pupils covered by the study

**Number of pupils in public sector education covered by the study (thousands)
and percentage of total enrolment (Public and Private)**

	ISCED 1		ISCED 2		ISCED 3	
	Number	%	Number	%	Number	%
Austria	356	96	319	93	360	90
Belgium	318	43	261	34[1]		
Denmark	309	91	212	88	61	
Finland	387	99	192	97	197	92
France	3 492	85	2 562	80	1 138	79
Germany	2 517	98	3 431	97	2 394	94
Ireland	411	98	201	100	144	100
Netherlands	452	31	134	19	47	24
New Zealand	307	98	97	95	217	95
Norway	467	100	[2]	100	198	96
Portugal	979	94	380	93	113	95
Spain	3 176	65[2]			1 962	73
Sweden	574	99	301	99	281	99
Switzerland	395	98	256	95	262	95
United States	40 900	89[3]				

1. ISCED 2 + ISCED 3.
2. ISCED 1 + ISCED 2.
3. ISCED 1 + ISCED 2 + ISCED 3.
Source: Data supplied in the replies to the questionnaires, subsequent to the verification procedure.

Importance of the various levels in the decision-making process according to the different trial systems of weighting

(ISCED 2, Public)

These different systems of weighting are described and commented on in the main body of the report. Different systems of weighting were tested in order to determine whether the evaluation of a country's decision-making process would vary significantly depending on the weight assigned to each of the 34 decisions studied.

Six weighting systems were tried out:

1. Each of the four fields is assigned equal weight. This means that, in fields containing a large number of decisions, each individual decision has a lower weight than those in other fields. This system of weighting is the one that was finally adopted and that served as the basis for the results set out in Part II of this study.
2. The field of resource allocation is assigned a coefficient of one and the three others a coefficient of two. Within each field, the decisions are assigned a coefficient of from one to two, depending on their "importance".
3. Each decision is assigned a coefficient of from one to four depending on its proximity to the pupil's actual educational situation.
4. Each decision is assigned a coefficient of from one to four depending on its proximity to the variables connected with the effectiveness of schools and classes.
5. Coefficients are assigned to the decisions within each field as per Method 3, with each of the four fields then being assigned an equal weight as per Method 1.
6. All decisions are assigned the same weight.

Decision-making levels: Weighting system 1

	School	Lower interm.	Upper interm.	Central gov.
Austria	37.6	7.8	26.2	28.5
Belgium	25.3	50.3	24.4	
Denmark	40.7	44.1		15.3
Finland	39.7	47.3		12.9
France	31.1		36.2	32.7
Germany[1]	32.6	42.2	18.4	6.8
Ireland	72.8	8.0		19.2
New Zealand	71.4			28.6
Norway	32.2	45.2		22.6
Portugal	39.5		3.2	57.3
Spain	27.6	26.1	13.3	33.1
Sweden	48.1	48.4		3.6
Switzerland	9.4	40.2	50.4	
United States	25.7	70.8	3.6	
Total	38.1	30.7	12.5	18.6

1. In Germany, the school takes 32.6 per cent of the 34 decisions studied, while the lower intermediate level takes 42.2 per cent of them.

Decision-making levels: Weighting system 2

	School	Lower interm.	Upper interm.	Central gov.
Austria	36.6	5.5	22.7	35.2
Belgium	26.5	51.2	22.3	
Denmark	42.0	36.6		21.4
Finland	42.8	39.0		18.2
France	31.1		29.2	39.7
Germany	36.4	35.5	17.4	10.7
Ireland	72.5	5.8		21.8
New Zealand	77.8			22.2
Norway	30.4	39.5		30.1
Portugal	37.4		4.7	57.9
Spain	31.1	18.0	13.6	37.3
Sweden	46.7	47.6		5.7
Switzerland	9.5	31.7	58.8	
United States	27.9	66.4	5.7	
Total	39.2	26.9	12.4	21.4

Decision-making levels: Weighting system 3

	School	Lower interm.	Upper interm.	Central gov.
Austria	44.0	5.0	18.7	32.3
Belgium	29.8	50.5	19.8	
Denmark	50.6	29.6		19.8
Finland	46.3	37.8		15.9
France	35.4		23.6	41.1
Germany	39.5	30.2	24.1	6.2
Ireland	74.0	4.7		21.4
New Zealand	79.3			20.7
Norway	34.6	34.6		30.8
Portugal	41.3		3.7	55.0
Spain	35.9	14.4	13.5	36.5
Sweden	54.9	40.2		4.9
Switzerland	15.7	27.1	57.1	
United States	34.1	61.0	4.9	
Total	44.3	24.0	11.3	20.4

Decision-making levels: Weighting system 4

	School	Lower interm.	Upper interm.	Central gov.
Austria	43.7	5.3	22.5	28.5
Belgium	27.3	50.4	22.3	
Denmark	46.1	35.5		18.4
Finland	39.0	45.5		15.6
France	34.2		22.5	43.3
Germany	35.5	33.6	24.3	6.6
Ireland	72.9	5.6		21.5
New Zealand	79.2			20.8
Norway	31.5	41.1		27.4
Portugal	38.8		5.2	56.0
Spain	35.6	16.4	15.1	32.9
Sweden	51.9	42.9		5.2
Switzerland	13.6	33.3	53.0	
United States	30.7	64.1	5.2	
Total	41.8	26.7	11.7	19.8

Decision-making levels: Weighting system 5

	School	Lower interm.	Upper interm.	Central gov.
Austria	44.2	4.1	15.6	36.1
Belgium	31.2	49.3	19.4	
Denmark	52.0	27.4		20.7
Finland	48.1	37.1		14.9
France	35.5		25.3	39.2
Germany	41.0	29.3	25.2	4.5
Ireland	74.8	4.5		20.7
New Zealand	75.7			24.3
Norway	38.8	31.6		29.7
Portugal	39.7		3.8	56.5
Spain	34.8	13.4	11.6	40.2
Sweden	56.0	38.3		5.7
Switzerland	13.5	24.9	61.7	
United States	35.5	58.8	5.7	
Total	44.3	22.7	12.1	20.9

Decision-making levels: Weighting system 6

	School	Lower interm.	Upper interm.	Central gov.
Austria	35.5	9.7	28.2	26.6
Belgium	22.9	52.9	24.1	
Denmark	39.4	45.5		15.2
Finland	38.2	47.1		14.7
France	30.4		33.3	36.3
Germany	30.3	42.4	18.2	9.1
Ireland	72.4	7.8		19.9
New Zealand	76.5			23.5
Norway	27.3	48.5		24.2
Portugal	40.9		2.9	56.2
Spain	27.3	27.3	15.2	30.3
Sweden	47.1	50.0		2.9
Switzerland	10.7	42.9	46.4	
United States	24.5	72.5	2.9	
Total	37.8	31.8	11.7	18.7

Annex 3

Detailed results

Table 3.1   Modes of decision-making in education systems
           a) public
           b) private

Table 3.2   Fields of decision-making for the four levels of the structure by ISCED level (Public).

Table 3.3   Country replies, item by item, for ISCED 2 public 1990/91 (synoptic tables).

Table 3.4   Proportion of decisions by level and by mode, by country and by ISCED level (public and private).

Notes: A table is supplied for private education only insofar as the country concerned has replied about it in the questionnaire. A reply was required only if private education accounted for over 5 per cent of the pupils concerned.

To round off the figures, the totals along the lines and down the columns may not be accurate to within one tenth.

Table 3.1*a.* **Modes of decision-making in education systems (Public)**

	Autonomy			Consultation			Set framework		
	ISCED 1	ISCED 2	ISCED 3	ISCED 1	ISCED 2	ISCED 3	ISCED 1	ISCED 2	ISCED 3
Austria	63	63	59	0	0	0	37	37	41
Belgium	64	58	58	5	10	10	31	33	33
Denmark	64	64	74	20	18	24	16	18	2
Finland	35	35	31	6	6	3	59	59	66
France	65	54	50	11	13	17	24	33	33
Germany [1]	42	42	42	21	21	21	37	37	37
Ireland	33	35	35	35	33	33	32	32	32
New Zealand	63	63	63	4	4	4	33	33	33
Norway	70	70	56	8	8	14	22	22	30
Portugal	56	63	63	21	8	8	23	29	29
Spain	58	58	55	14	14	15	28	28	30
Sweden	48	48	48	6	6	6	46	46	46
Switzerland	66	63	49	10	21	32	24	16	20
United States	19	19	19	44	44	44	37	37	37

1. In Germany, at each of the three stages, 42 per cent of the 34 decisions surveyed are taken autonomously, 21 per cent in conjunction with another level in the system, and 37 per cent within a framework set by a higher level.

Table 3.1*b.* **Modes of decision-making in education systems (Private)**

	Autonomy			Consultation			Set framework		
	ISCED 1	ISCED 2	ISCED 3	ISCED 1	ISCED 2	ISCED 3	ISCED 1	ISCED 2	ISCED 3
Austria	–	70	68	–	3	3	–	27	29
Belgium	64	59	59	14	17	17	22	24	24
France	80	63	63	4	11	11	16	26	26
Portugal	77	72	77	0	0	0	23	28	23
Spain	62	62	77	4	4	2	34	34	21
United States	66	66	66	6	6	6	28	28	28

Table 3.2.   **Fields of decision-making at the four levels of the structure by ISCED level (Public)** [1]

	N	OI	PS	PM	RA	Proportion of decisions taken
School						
ISCED 1	14	56	16	15	13	35
ISCED 2	14	52	18	15	16	38
ISCED 3	14	50	17	16	17	41
Lower intermediate (LI)						
ISCED 1*	12	8	17	32	43	35
ISCED 2	11	7	16	35	42	31
ISCED 3	8	6	22	32	40	19
Upper intermediate (UI)						
ISCED 1	7	13	32	30	26	10
ISCED 2	8	15	33	23	28	12
ISCED 3	10	8	25	30	37	21
National						
ISCED 1	11	8	52	27	13	20
ISCED 2	11	7	49	30	14	19
ISCED 3	12	9	44	32	14	19

*   For ISCED 1, decisions are taken at level LI in 12 countries. Overall, decisions taken at this level account for 35 per cent of the decision-making structure, 43 per cent of the 35 per cent (or approximately 15 per cent) are taken in the resource allocation field.

1.   OI   = Organisation of instruction
     PS   = Planning and structures
     PM = Personnel management
     RA = Resource allocation.

Table 3.3. **Country replies, item by item, for ISCED 2 public, 1990-91 (synoptic tables)**[1]

a) Organisation of instruction

	School	Lower intermediate	Upper intermediate	National	No answer
P1 Bodies determining the school attended	BEL, FRA (0.5), GER, IRE, NZL, OST, SPA	DEN, FIN, NOR, SWE, USA	FRA (0.5), POR, SWI		
P2 Decisions affecting school careers	All countries except NOR, SWI		SWI		NOR
P3 Length of schooling time	DEN, IRE, NZL, SWE, USA (0.5)	NOR, USA (0.5)	BEL, GER, SWI	FIN, FRA, POR, SPA	OST
P4 Selection of school books	BEL, DEN, FIN, FRA,GER, IRE, NZL, OST, POR, SPA, SWE, USA (0.5)	USA (0.5)	SWI		
P5 Methods of grouping pupils	BEL (0.4) and all other countries except SWI	BEL (0.6)	SWI		
P6 The organisation of aid for school work	All countries except FIN, IRE	FIN		IRE	
P7 Teaching methods	BEL (0.4) and all other countries	BEL (0.6)			
P8 Methods of evaluating pupils' normal work	All countries				

Table 3.3. **Country replies, item by item, for ISCED 2 public, 1990-91 (synoptic tables)**[1] *(cont'd)*

b) Planning and structures

	School	Lower intermediate	Upper intermediate	National	No answer
S1 Creation and closure of schools	IRE (0.8)	BEL, DAN, FIN, GER, IRE (0.2), NOR, SWE, USA	FRA, OST (0.75), SPA (0.5), SWI,	NZL, OST (0.25) , POR, SPA (0.5)	
S3 Planning of courses on the basis of subject matters	FIN, IRE, NZL	BEL, USA (0.5)	GER, SWI	DEN, FRA, NOR, OST, POR, SPA,	
S41 Choice of range of subject matters	GER, IRE, NZL, SWE, USA (0.5)	BEL, USA (0.5)	SWI	DEN, FIN, FRA, NOR, OST, POR, SPA	
S42 Choice of range of courses	DEN, FIN, IRE, NZL	BEL, GER, SWE, USA	FRA, SWI	NOR, OST, POR, SPA	
S5 Course content	DEN, IRE, NOR, OST, SWE, USA (0.5)	BEL, FIN, USA (0.5)	SPA (0.5), SWI	FRA, NZL, POR, SPA (0.5)	
S6 Structure and content of qualifying examinations	BEL (0.4), FIN	BEL (0.6)	GER, USA	DEN, FRA, IRE, NOR, NZL, POR, SWE	OST, SPA, SWI
S7 Credentialling	BEL, DEN, FIN, GER, NOR, POR, SWE, USA (0.5)	USA (0.5)	FRA	IRE, NZL	OST, SPA, SWI

96

Table 3.3. **Country replies, item by item, for ISCED 2 public, 1990-91 (synoptic tables)[1]** *(cont'd)*

c) Personnel management

	School	Lower intermediate	Upper intermediate	National	No answer
R1 Hiring or dismissal of staff					
1. School principal	IRE (0.75), NZL, POR, SPA	BEL, DEN, FIN, GER, IRE (0.25), NOR, SWE, SWI, USA	OST	FRA	
2. Teachers	IRE (0.75), NZL	BEL, DEN, FIN, GER, IRE (0.25), NOR, SWE, SWI, USA	FRA (0.5), OST, SPA (0.5)	FRA (0.5), POR, SPA (0.5)	
3. Others	IRE (0.75), NZL, USA (0.5)	BEL, DEN, FIN, GER IRE (0.25), NOR, OST (0.75), SPA, SWE, SWI, USA (0.5)	FRA, OST (0.25)	POR	
R2 Duties and conditions of service					
1. School principal	FIN, IRE (0.75), NZL, POR,	BEL, DEN, GER (0.5), IRE (0.25), SWE, SWI, USA	GER (0.5), SPA(0.5)	IRE, NOR, OST, SPA (0.5)	
2. Teachers	DEN, FIN, FRA, IRE, NZL, POR, SWE	BEL, GER, SWI, USA	SPA (0.5)	IRE, NOR, OST, SPA (0.5)	
3. Others	DEN, FIN, FRA, IRE, NZL, POR, SWE	BEL, GER (0.5), NOR, OST (0.75), SPA, SWI, USA	GER (0.5), OST (0.25)		
R3 Setting salary levels					
1. School principal	NZL	SWE, USA	BEL, SPA (0.5), SWI	DEN, FIN, FRA, GER, IRE, NOR, OST, POR, SPA (0.5)	
2. Teachers	NZL	SWE, USA	BEL, SPA (0.5), SWI	DEN, FIN, FRA, GER, IRE, NOR, OST, POR, SPA (0.5)	
3. Others	IRE, NZL	DEN, NOR, SPA, SWE, USA	BEL	FIN, FRA, GER, POR	OST, SWI

Table 3.3. **Country replies, item by item, for ISCED 2 public, 1990-91 (synoptic tables)** [1] *(cont'd)*

d) Resources

	School	Lower intermediate	Upper intermediate	National	No answer
F1 Allocation of resources for:					
1. Teaching staff		DEN, FIN, IRE (0.25), GER, NOR, SWE, SWI, USA	BEL, SPA (0.5), FRA, OST	IRE (0.75), NZL, POR, SPA (0.5)	
2. Other staff	IRE (0.75)	DEN, FIN, GER, IRE (0.25), NOR, OST (0.75), SPA, SWE, SWI, USA	BEL, FRA, OST (0.25)	NZL, POR	
3. Capital expenditure	IRE (0.75), POR (0.3)	BEL (0.4), DEN, FIN, GER, IRE (0.25), NOR, SPA, SWE, SWI, USA	BEL (0.6), FRA, OST	NZL, POR (0.7)	
4. Operating expenditure	IRE (0.75), POR (0.3)	BEL (0.4), DEN, FIN, GER, IRE (0.25), NOR, SPA, SWE, SWI, USA	BEL (0.6), FRA, OST	NZL, POR (0.7)	
F2 Utilisation of resources by the school:					
1. Staff	DEN, FRA, IRE, NOR, NZL OST, SWE	FIN, GER, SPA, SWI, USA	BEL	POR	
2. Capital expenditure	IRE (0.75), NZL, OST, POR	BEL, DEN, FIN, GER, IRE (0.24), NOR, SPA, SWE, SWI, USA	FRA		
3. Operating expenditure	BEL (0.6), FIN, FRA, GER, IRE (0.75), NOR, NZL, OST, POR (0.3), SPA, SWE	BEL (0.4), DEN, IRE (0.25), USA	SWI	POR (0.7)	

1. In France, for about half the pupils at ISCED 2 public, the school can be chosen by their families. For the other half, the LI determines which school to attend.

Table 3.4. **Proportion of decisions by level and by mode, by country and by ISCED level**
(Public and Private)
AUSTRIA

	School	Int. I	Int. II	State	Total
ISCED 1 public					
Autonomy	13.4	10.4	11.7	27.2	62.7
Consultation					
Set framework	24.2		13.1		37.3
Total	37.6	10.4	24.8	27.2	100.0
ISCED 2 public					
Autonomy	14.3	7.8	12.8	28.5	63.4
Consultation					
Set framework	23.3		13.3		36.6
Total	37.6	7.8	26.2	28.5	100.0
ISCED 3 public					
Autonomy	15.4	4.5	16.4	22.9	59.2
Consultation					
Set framework	26.2		14.6		40.8
Total	41.6	4.5	30.9	22.9	100.0
ISCED 2 private					
Autonomy	41.1		2.0	27.2	70.3
Consultation	3.1				3.1
Set framework	22.1		4.5		26.6
Total	66.2		6.5	27.2	100.0
ISCED 3 private					
Autonomy	38.1		3.6	26.5	68.2
Consultation	3.1				3.1
Set framework	24.2		4.5		28.7
Total	65.4		8.1	26.5	100.0

BELGIUM

	School	Int. I	Int. II	State	Total
ISCED 1 public					
Autonomy	25.0	15.3	23.8		64.1
Consultation		4.7			4.7
Set framework	3.3	27.9			31.2
Total	28.3	47.9	23.8		100.0
ISCED 2 public					
Autonomy	21.9	11.3	24.4		57.6
Consultation		9.5			9.5
Set framework	3.4	29.5			32.9
Total	25.3	50.3	24.4		100.0
ISCED 3 public					
Autonomy	21.9	11.3	24.4		57.6
Consultation		9.5			9.5
Set framework	3.4	29.5			32.9
Total	25.3	50.3	24.4		100.0
ISCED 1 private					
Autonomy	36.5		27.2		63.7
Consultation	13.9				13.9
Set framework	22.4				22.4
Total	72.8		27.2		100.0
ISCED 2 private					
Autonomy	32.1		27.3		59.4
Consultation	17.0				17.0
Set framework	23.6				23.6
Total	72.7		27.3		100.0
ISCED 3 private					
Autonomy	32.1		27.3		59.4
Consultation	17.0				17.0
Set framework	23.6				23.6
Total	72.7		27.3		100.0

DENMARK

	School	Int. I	Int. II	State	Total
ISCED 1 public					
Autonomy	19.2	29.6		15.3	64.1
Consultation	9.0	11.4			20.3
Set framework	12.5	3.1			15.6
Total	40.7	44.1		15.3	100.0
ISCED 2 public					
Autonomy	19.2	29.6		15.3	64.0
Consultation	9.0	9.1			18.1
Set framework	12.5	5.4			17.9
Total	40.7	44.1		15.3	100.0
ISCED 3 public					
Autonomy	28.3		21.4	24.7	74.4
Consultation	14.8		9.1		23.8
Set framework			1.8		1.8
Total	43.0		32.3	24.7	100.0

FINLAND

	School	Int. I	Int. II	State	Total
ISCED 1 public					
Autonomy	19.7	5.7		9.8	35.1
Consultation		6.2			6.2
Set framework	23.2	35.5			58.7
Total	42.8	47.3		9.8	100.0
ISCED 2 public					
Autonomy	19.7	2.1		12.9	34.7
Consultation		6.3			6.3
Set framework	20.1	39.0			59.1
Total	39.7	47.3		12.9	100.0
ISCED 3 public					
Autonomy	17.7	1.0		12.0	30.7
Consultation		3.1			3.1
Set framework	42.1	24.0			66.2
Total	59.8	28.2		12.0	100.0

FRANCE

	School	Int. I	Int. II	State	Total
ISCED 1 public					
Autonomy	10.4	22.2		32.3	64.9
Consultation		7.2	4.2		11.3
Set framework	6.3	6.3	11.3		23.8
Total	16.7	35.6	15.5	32.3	100.0
ISCED 2 public					
Autonomy	12.5		12.3	29.2	54.0
Consultation			9.9	3.5	13.4
Set framework	18.6		14.0		32.6
Total	31.1		36.2	32.7	100.0
ISCED 3 public					
Autonomy	12.5		11.6	26.3	50.4
Consultation			12.8	4.2	17.0
Set framework	18.6		14.0		32.6
Total	31.1		38.4	30.5	100.0
ISCED 1 private					
Autonomy	50.7	5.6		24.0	80.2
Consultation			4.2		4.2
Set framework	11.5		4.2		15.6
Total	62.2	5.6	8.3	24.0	100.0
ISCED 2 private					
Autonomy	44.2		2.4	15.9	62.5
Consultation	3.6		7.7		11.3
Set framework	15.5		10.7		26.2
Total	63.2		20.8	15.9	100.0
ISCED 3 private					
Autonomy	44.2		2.4	15.9	62.5
Consultation	3.6		7.7		11.3
Set framework	15.5		10.7		26.2
Total	63.2		20.8	15.9	100.0

GERMANY

	School	Int. I	Int. II	State	Total
ISCED 1 public					
Autonomy	3.1	14.1	18.4	6.8	42.4
Consultation	3.6	17.5			21.1
Set framework	25.9	10.6			36.5
Total	32.6	42.2	18.4	6.8	100.0
ISCED 2 public					
Autonomy	3.1	14.1	18.4	6.8	42.4
Consultation	3.6	17.5			21.1
Set framework	25.9	10.6			36.5
Total	32.6	42.2	18.4	6.8	100.0
ISCED 3 public					
Autonomy	3.1	14.4	18.4	6.8	42.4
Consultation	3.6	17.5			21.1
Set framework	25.9	10.6			36.5
Total	32.6	42.2	18.4	6.8	100.0

IRELAND

	School	Int. I	Int. II	State	Total
ISCED 1 public					
Autonomy	17.7			15.0	32.7
Consultation				35.3	35.3
Set framework	32.0				32.0
Total	49.7			50.3	100.0
ISCED 2 public					
Autonomy	20.9			14.0	34.9
Consultation	20.4	7.5		5.2	33.1
Set framework	31.5	0.5			32.0
Total	72.8	8.0		19.2	100.0
ISCED 3 public					
Autonomy	20.9			14.0	34.9
Consultation	20.4	7.5		5.2	33.1
Set framework	31.5	0.5			32.0
Total	72.8	8.0		19.2	100.0

NEW ZEALAND

	School	Int. I	Int. II	State	Total
ISCED 1 public					
Autonomy	38.4			25.0	63.4
Consultation				3.6	3.6
Set framework	33.0				33.0
Total	71.4			28.6	100.0
ISCED 2 public					
Autonomy	38.4			25.0	63.4
Consultation				3.6	3.6
Set framework	33.0				33.0
Total	71.4			28.6	100.0
ISCED 3 public					
Autonomy	45.5			17.9	63.4
Consultation				3.6	3.6
Set framework	33.0				33.0
Total	78.5			21.5	100.0

NORWAY

	School	Int. I	Int. II	State	Total
ISCED 1 public					
Autonomy	14.3	33.3		22.6	70.2
Consultation		8.3			8.3
Set framework	17.9	3.6			21.5
Total	32.2	45.2		22.6	100.0
ISCED 2 public					
Autonomy	14.3	33.3		22.6	70.2
Consultation		8.3			8.3
Set framework	17.9	3.6			21.5
Total	32.2	45.2		22.6	100.0
ISCED 3 public					
Autonomy	6.7		27.2	22.2	56.1
Consultation			14.0		14.0
Set framework	19.7		10.3		29.9
Total	26.4		51.5	22.2	100.0

PORTUGAL

	School	Int. I	Int. II	State	Total
ISCED 1 public					
Autonomy	9.4	0.4		45.9	55.6
Consultation	1.6	17.8		2.1	21.4
Set framework	19.7	3.2			22.9
Total	30.6	21.4		48.0	100.0
ISCED 2 public					
Autonomy	9.4			53.8	63.1
Consultation	1.6		3.2	3.6	8.3
Set framework	28.6				28.6
Total	39.5		3.2	57.3	100.0
ISCED 3 public					
Autonomy	9.4			53.8	63.1
Consultation	1.6		3.2	3.6	8.3
Set framework	28.6				28.6
Total	39.5		3.2	57.3	100.0
ISCED 1 private					
Autonomy	58.8			17.9	76.7
Consultation					
Set framework	23.3				23.3
Total	82.1			17.9	100.0
ISCED 2 private					
Autonomy	59.4			12.5	71.9
Consultation					
Set framework	28.1				28.1
Total	87.5			12.5	100.0
ISCED 3 private					
Autonomy	58.8			17.9	76.7
Consultation					
Set framework	23.3				23.3
Total	82.1			17.9	100.0

SPAIN

	School	Int. I	Int. II	State	Total
ISCED 1 public					
Autonomy	9.8	11.9	4.9	31.0	57.6
Consultation	3.1	7.1	2.1	2.1	14.4
Set framework	14.6	7.1	6.3		28.0
Total	27.6	26.1	13.3	33.1	100.0
ISCED 2 public					
Autonomy	9.8	11.9	4.9	31.0	57.6
Consultation	3.1	7.1	2.1	2.1	14.4
Set framework	14.6	7.1	6.3		28.0
Total	27.6	26.1	13.3	33.1	100.0
ISCED 3 public					
Autonomy	12.9		8.8	32.8	54.5
Consultation		7.1	4.1	4.1	15.4
Set framework	14.6	7.1	8.4		30.1
Total	27.5	14.2	21.3	36.9	100.0
ISCED 1 private					
Autonomy	40.3			21.9	62.2
Consultation		3.6			3.6
Set framework	25.1	7.1	2.1		34.3
Total	65.3	10.7	2.1	21.9	100.0
ISCED 2 private					
Autonomy	40.3			21.9	62.2
Consultation		3.6			3.6
Set framework	25.1	7.1	2.1		34.3
Total	65.3	10.7	2.1	21.9	100.0
ISCED 3 private					
Autonomy	59.7			17.7	77.4
Consultation		1.8			1.8
Set framework	15.1	3.6	2.1		20.8
Total	74.8	5.4	2.1	17.7	100.0

SWEDEN

	School	Int. I	Int. II	State	Total
ISCED 1 public					
Autonomy	14.6	29.7		3.6	47.9
Consultation		6.3			6.3
Set framework	33.5	12.4			45.8
Total	48.1	48.4		3.6	100.0
ISCED 2 public					
Autonomy	14.6	29.7		3.6	47.9
Consultation		6.3			6.3
Set framework	33.5	12.4			45.8
Total	48.1	48.4		3.6	100.0
ISCED 3 public					
Autonomy	14.6	29.7		3.6	47.9
Consultation		6.3			6.3
Set framework	33.5	12.4			45.8
Total	48.1	48.4		3.6	100.0

SWITZERLAND

	School	Int. I	Int. II	State	Total
ISCED 1 public					
Autonomy		33.9	32.5		66.4
Consultation		3.6	6.3		9,8
Set framework	9.4	14.4			23.7
Total	9.4	51.9	38.8		100.0
ISCED 2 public					
Autonomy		33.9	29.4		63.3
Consultation			21.1		21.1
Set framework	9.4	6.2			15.6
Total	9.4	40.2	50.4		100.0
ISCED 3 public					
Autonomy	5.6		43.1		48.8
Consultation	5.6		14.8	11.3	31.8
Set framework	9.4		10.1		19.5
Total	20.7		68.0	11.3	100.0

UNITED STATES

	School	Int. I	Int. II	State	Total
ISCED 1 public					
Autonomy	5.2	10.2	3.6		18.9
Consultation	1.2	43.0			44.2
Set framework	19.3	17.5			36.8
Total	25.7	70.8	3.6		100.0
ISCED 2 public					
Autonomy	5.2	10.2	3.6		18.9
Consultation	1.2	43.0			44.2
Set framework	19.3	17.5			36.8
Total	25.7	70.8	3.6		100.0
ISCED 3 public					
Autonomy	5.2	10.2	3.6		18.9
Consultation	1.2	43.0			44.2
Set framework	19.3	17.5			36.8
Total	25.7	70.8	3.6		100.0
ISCED 1 private					
Autonomy	66.2				66.2
Consultation	3.8	2.4			6.1
Set framework	25.3	2.4			27.7
Total	95.3	4.7			100.0
ISCED 2 private					
Autonomy	66.2				66.2
Consultation	3.8	2.4			6.1
Set framework	25.3	2.4			27.7
Total	95.3	4.7			100.0
ISCED 3 private					
Autonomy	66.2				66.2
Consultation	3.8	2.4			6.1
Set framework	25.3	2.4			27.7
Total	95.3	4.7			100.0

Annex 4

Questionnaire and descriptive matrix

The locus of decision-making in national education systems

(Explanatory note to the descriptive matrix)

Some education systems are considered centralised and others decentralised whereas, in fact, the extent to which a system is centralised (*i.e.* the proximity to the centre of the locus where major decisions are taken) may differ depending on the aspect concerned.

For example, under the French education system, which is considered to be highly centralised, teachers are free to choose their own textbooks on a market which is not controlled in any way by the State.

What is more, the trends in this respect also differ depending on the aspect concerned.

In most countries what we are seeing now is an increasing centralisation of decisions or specifications with regard to curricula and examinations, coupled with a greater measure of autonomy for schools in other areas. The developments taking place in the various countries are the result of a deliberate and explicit policy on the part of the authorities aimed at improving the efficiency of their education systems.

It has never been proved experimentally that one particular decision-making structure was more "efficient" than another. However, this structure is one of the more malleable variables that governments can influence, and they change it fairly frequently to a more or less radical extent.

When making such changes the structures in foreign countries are often quoted as examples. In most cases such comparisons are confined to the particular decision in question, without this being placed in the context of the structure as a whole, which necessarily limits the relevance and significance of the comparison.

This is why it was felt that it was important, in the case of a project designed to compare national education systems, to include among the characteristics of the systems a number of indicators denoting their degree of centralisation, and that these indicators should be constructed on the basis of a thorough, systematic and comprehensive analysis of the main decision-making processes or lines of authority involved in the operation of education systems.

This is the purpose of the descriptive matrix presented below, which is made up of four data sheets covering:

1. Organisation of instruction.
2. Planning and structures.
3. Personnel management.
4. Resources allocation and use.

Each data sheet is subdivided into a number of "items", each relating to a more specific type of responsibility (*e.g.* the hiring of staff in the case of Data Sheet 3). For each of these items the data sheet indicates as explained below at what level a decision is taken (*i.e.* the school, central government or some intermediate level).

This annex contains:

1. A number of principles underlying the way the data sheets have been set out and which need to be understood in order to fill them in correctly.
2. Instructions as to how to describe a decision-making process on the data sheet.
3. The method for combining where necessary the basic data sheets onto one consolidated data sheet for the country as a whole.
4. Details of the final consolidation to be carried out by the Franco-Swiss Working Party and of the indicators that will be constructed.

Principles underlying the way the descriptive matrix has been laid out

a) It was first of all agreed that Member countries, when using the proposed matrix, would confine themselves to a DESCRIPTION OF THE LEGAL which may sometimes be quite different from the practical reality. However in cases where some formal allocation of authority is manifestly disregarded, countries should mention this in a note.

b) SCOPE OF THE STUDY: pre-primary and special education are not covered. These two types of education are organised in a way very different from that for mainstream education and an analysis of these could therefore be postponed until a later date.

In addition, it was agreed to confine this study to ISCED levels 1, 2 and 3 – the format of the matrix and the items covered are not entirely suitable for the other levels, *i.e.* ISCED levels 5, 6 and 7.

c) TERMINOLOGY: before giving details as to how the proposed matrix should be used, the terms of employed need to be defined.

– **Basic system**: this is a system governed by the same set of rules. In other words, in order for 2 subsets to be considered as two distinct basic systems, their method of operation must differ in at least one fundamental respect.

Example: In France, first level and second level public education form two basic systems, chiefly because their teaching staff are not administered at the same level and first level schools have far less autonomy.

A change from one basic system to another may therefore occur as a result of a change in ISCED level and/or region and/or legal status.

– **Regional administrative units**: these would be the cantons in Switzerland, the Länder in Germany, the states in the USA and the provinces in Canada. Each regional administrative unit may have its own particular system of education which would have to be described on a separate basic data sheet.

– **Education levels based on the ISCED classification:** given the wide variety of levels within the different education systems, it was considered preferable to use this work "level" in the ISCED meaning of the term, where the classification is based on three simple criteria: the duration of schooling prior to entry to this level, the duration of

110

education at this level, and where applicable, the type of qualification awarded on completion of this level.

For our purposes we have taken three ISCED levels. A consolidated data sheet will be compiled for each of these levels, combining the various basic data sheets for this level for those countries that have opted for the detailed method.

1. First level education (ISCED level 1)

This level starts at age 5, 6 or 7 and lasts 5-6 years.

2. Second level-first stage (ISCED level 2)

The second level-first stage starts at age 11 or 12 and lasts 3-4 years. It is also known as lower secondary education.

It usually coincides with the end of compulsory education. In most countries it consists of general education, although in some cases there is also a pre-vocational stream which however is not really designed to provide students with occupational or job training.

3. Second level-second stage (ISCED level 3)

The second level-second stage starts at age 14 to 16 and consists of 3-4 years of full-time education.

It includes general education, teacher training and vocational/technical education for students who have completed the second level-first stage. It can be either the end of a person's formal education prior to starting working life or a preparation for entry to third level education.

Each of the three levels described above will be analyzed on the basis of the matrix for the locus of decision-making. ISCED levels 5, 6 and 7 could be analyzed subsequently using a different matrix more suited to the situation in their case.

Instructions on how to fill the matrix for "The locus of decision-making in national education systems"

The matrix comprises 21 items representing the main activities involved in the operation of an education system.

The matrix is divided into four parts:
- Planning structures (items S1 to S7).
- Organisation of instruction (items P1 to P8).
- Personnel management (items R1 to R4).
- Resources (items F1 and F2).

Note: An item may be subdivided in order to show different situations under the same heading.

For each of these items what must be indicated is how and by whom the corresponding decision is taken.

The matrix is accordingly divided into 6 columns:
- the first column on the left contains the list of items;
- the second column (Level 1) is for the school;

- the third column (Level 2) is for the decision-making level institutionally *closest to the school*;
- the fourth column (Level 3) is for the intermediate decision-making level *closest to central government*;
- the fifth column (Level 4) is for the decision-making level institutionally furthest from the school, *i.e. Central Government (national or federal)*;
- the sixth column is for comments.

There is thus a progression from the level of the school to the level of central government corresponding to the degree of closeness between the school and a particular institutional decision-making level, *e.g.* the school is closer to the local authority (which will therefore usually be Level 2) than to the region (in France), the *Land* (in Germany) or the canton (in Switzerland) which will figure in Level 3.

Depending on the administrative and policy-making structure in each country one, two or three columns should be used, and extra columns should be added if necessary.

The place where the decision relating to the item concerned is taken is indicated by the letters A, B, C.

"A" means that the decision is taken entirely at this level (full autonomy);

"B" means that the decision is taken at this level but jointly or after consultation with another authority;

"C" means that the decision is taken at this level but within a framework established by another authority (limited autonomy) this framework may be legal, administrative or financial.

The letters A, B, C indicate the decision-making level, but other levels are involved in the process in the case of B and C.

This will be shown by using the following signs:

"-" means that this level is not in any way involved in the decision-making process;

"?" means that for one reason or another, no reply can be given in this case;

"b" means that this level is consulted or participates in making the decision;

"c" means that it is the level which has established the legal framework or the amount of funding affecting the decision taken by an authority.

Note: "b" and "c" are not incompatible, *i.e.* a decision may be taken within an established framework and also after consultation.

The signs A, B, -, b, c thus indicate the degree of involvement of each level in the decision-making process for each of the items.

However, in the case of the intermediate levels (Level 2 and Level 3) this will not indicate the nature of the authority concerned. If need be, this could be done by coupling the following letters to the letters A, B, C, b, c:

"e" for an *elected* authority or service answerable to it (*e.g.* local authority, schoolboard, etc.);

"i" for an *intermediate* service or agency answerable to central government (*e.g.* regional offices of a Ministry of Education);

"p" for a *private* body.

Countries where one of the intermediate levels does not exist should indicate this by crossing out the corresponding column.

Examples:

Table 4.1.

Item	Level 1 School	Level 2	Level 3	Level 4 Central government
Item	–	–		A

This means that the decision is taken wholly by central government (national or federal) without consultation. There is only one intermediate level.

Table 4.2.

Item	Level 1 School	Level 2	Level 3	Level 4 Central government
Item	b	Bp	–	–

This means that the decision is taken by a private authority close to the school either jointly or in consultation with the school.

Table 4.3.

Item	Level 1 School	Level 2	Level 3	Level 4 Central government
Item	C	–	ci	–

This means that the decision is taken by the school as one of a series of decisions which it has been empowered to take by a regional agency of central government or in connection with a grant made to it by that agency.

Table 4.4.

Item	Level 1 School	Level 2	Level 3	Level 4 Central government
Item	b	–	Bec	c

This means that the decision is taken by an elected regional authority after consultation with the school but in accordance with a binding legal framework established by central government.

In the case of a centralised education system the instructions given above are all that are needed for filing in the three data sheets (ISCED 1, 2 and 3) describing the system.

The additional instructions given hereunder are intended for countries which have a number of parallel systems where decisions are taken at different levels.

Method of aggregation

At the outset countries may opt for either of the following two alternatives.

The global method

Those countries where it would be far too complicated to fill in individual basic data sheets can choose a more simple global method that will provide at least a realistic, if not a detailed, picture of their education system.

Countries choosing this method can save themselves the trouble of having to fill in numerous basic data sheets by calling a meeting of a selected group of persons with specialist knowledge of the structure and operation of each of the three ISCED concerned (ISCED 1, ISCED 2 and ISCED 3). It will be up to this "brains trust", after consultation, to fill in the decision-making matrices for these three ISCED levels concerned *using the threshhold method* that is to say:

- if, for a given item, a particular procedure applies to 65 per cent or more of the total school population at this level, only one letter denoting this majority procedure should be entered in the column;
- if, for a given item, two different procedures apply in the ISCED level concerned, each covering 35 per cent or more of the school population in that level, then a letter denoting these practices should be entered in each of the two columns concerned;
- lastly, in the case where, for a given item, a number of different practices apply, each of which covers less than 35 per cent of the total school population in the level concerned, the words "different practices" should be entered against this item.

The detailed method

Using this detailed method the *first step* will be to establish basic data sheets, that is to say to fill in n decision-making matrices, *i.e.* three data sheets, one for each of the ISCED levels concerned multiplied by y basic systems (there is no need to fill in a data sheet for small basic systems covering less than 5 per cent of the total school population in the ISCED level concerned).

These n basic matrices, describing in detail the locus of decision-making in each country's education system, will then need to be combined together into consolidated data sheets showing the internal organisation of each country's education system.

The *second step* therefore will involve combining the basic data sheets into three consolidated data sheets, one for each ISCED level.

This consolidation should be done by taking the two most frequently used procedures for each item. Each procedure should be denoted by the corresponding letter plus the number of pupils concerned (in thousands) within the system in question.

Example: A country with five basic systems at ISCED 2 procedure for entering data under item P1:

SE1 covers 20 000 pupils;
SE2 covers 20 000 pupils;
SE3 covers 30 000 pupils;
SE4 covers 26 000 pupils;
SE5 covers 4 000 pupils.
(SE = Basic System)

No basic data sheet needs to be filled in for SE5. In addition, SE1 and SE2 have the same decision-making procedure for item P1.

The consolidated data sheet should mention only the two most frequently used decision-making procedures, *i.e.* SE1 and SE2 combined and SE3.

The consolidated data sheet for P1 would therefore be as follows.

P1   "Who decides what school a child should attend?"

	Level 1 School	Level 2	Level 3	Level 4 Central government
P1	A 30 C 40	Ce 40	–	–

Separated consolidated data sheets should be made out for public sector and private sector systems, except of course in the case of countries where the number of pupils in the private sector account for less than 5 per cent of the total school population.

Final consolidation

A final consolidated matrix will be compiled once Network C Member countries have sent in the data sheets describing the decision-making process.

What will be done will be to calculate for each country and for the total of all items combined on each of the four data sheets comprising the matrix (Organisation of Instruction, Personnel Management, etc.) the proportion of decisions take in full autonomy (A), jointly (B) and in limited autonomy (C), indicating the percentage of the total school population covered by a particular decision-making procedure.

Once this has been done for each of the countries sending in consolidated data sheets, it will then be possible to compare the situation as regards the different education systems. The outcome of this will take the form of a comparative table (see Table 4.5.) showing for each of the countries concerned the way in which decisions are taken (A full autonomy, B jointly, C limited autonomy) at each of the three levels (School, Intermediate level, Central government).

115

Table 4.5. **Organisation of instruction**

	Level 1 School (%)		Level 2 (%)		Level 4 Central government (%)	
SYLDAVIE	A	0	A	0	A	20
	B	0	B	0	B	0
	C	60	C	20	C	0
BORDURIE	A	10	A	10	A	0
	B	0	B	0	B	0
	C	50	C	30	C	0
MAREMMA	A	30	A	0	A	50
	B	0	B	10	B	0
	C	10	C	0	C	0
MONTAGNA	A	57	A	0	A	16
	B	0	B	27	B	0
	C	10	C	0	C	0

In addition, *two indicators* will be calculated and incorporated among the other indicators in the INES Project. These will be:

  a) the school's degree of autonomy (that is to say the proportion of decisions taken independently by the school *i.e.* the proportion of As among all of the capital letters denoting decisions in column 1);

  b) the degree of joint decision-making (that is to say the proportion of decisions taken jointly, *i.e.* the proportion of Bs among all the capital letters denoting decisions).

For each country, these indicators will be calculated for the following categories of schools:

public   ISCED level 1

public   ISCED level 2

public   ISCED level 1 + 2

public   ISCED level 3

private   ISCED level 1

private   ISCED level 2

private   ISCED level 1 + 2

private   ISCED level 3

Data sheets describing these indicators will be submitted to members of the Network at the March 1991 meeting.

The locus of decision-making in educational systems

Ministère de l'Éducation nationale et de la Culture
Direction de l'Évaluation et de la Prospective, Paris

In order to avoid, as far as possible, bias coming from misunderstanding between the respondents and the people who created the questionnaire, here is a list of some of the questionnaire's items with additional details. It is important to note that these items give more details, and do not modify, the former items. The footnotes of the former definitions, for example, remain valid.

P2   Decisions affecting pupils' orientation:
These decisions take place at the end of the year or at the end of a cycle: to repeat a grade, to change discipline or to transfer. They may be taken at school level, but also at a higher level, if they take into account the deliberations of a commission, or an examination organised by this higher level.
If these decisions are made differently, please answer those questions having the most important consequences, for the pupils.

P3   Number of instruction hours received by a pupil per year.

P4   Mode of grouping pupils.
Is the school administration free to group pupils, or is it constrained by rules and regulations, defining the minimum or maximum size of the group, or the principles of grouping (heterogeneity or homogeneity of the group)?

P8   Method of assessing pupils' regular work.
This deals with periodical assessments, grading scale, exam content and nature. Examinations or tests which apply to several schools together are not taken into account.

S3   Programme design based on subject matter.
A "programme" is the set of subjects studied by a given pupil during a school year or an ISCED level. Who decides, and how, in a given programme the proportion of maths, mother language, etc.? **S3** deals with the respective weight of the different matters in the programmes, **S4-2** deals with the presence of the subject in the range of subjects taught in the school.

S4-1   Choice of subject matters taught in the school.
Does the school administration choose freely the subjects taught? If not, which level decides which subjects the school teaches, or the set of subjects among which the school may choose?

S4-2 Choice of programmes taught in the school.
If the curriculum is made up of codified programmes, who decides and how that a certain school teaches a certain programme? If you answered ''A/School'' to **S3** and **S4-1** then you have to answer the same to **S4-2**. If **S3** and **S4-2** are both decided on a higher level, **S4-1** is decided so too. But **S3**, may have a different answer from **S4-1** and **S4-2**.

S5 Defining the syllabus
Who decides, and how, what must be taught in for example mathematics per grade (objectives and topics)?

Note: The domain of curriculum is covered by items **P3, S3, S4-1, S4-2** and **S5**.

S6 Final exams for diplomas.
Who decides, and how, the subject matter for examinations ending a given cycle? Who decides, and how, the respective weight of the different subjects in the examination?

R1 Hiring and firing of staff.
This decision deals with the choice of the person who will hold a given post: Mr. Smith rather than Mrs. Martin as a mathematics teacher, for example. The choice between a teacher of mathematics and a secretary is described in **F2-1**. The choice between a teacher in mathematics and teachers in history is described in **S3** or in **F2-1**.

R2 Terms of service and duties of staff.
Terms of service include duties (the minimum amount of hours which has to be worked per week or per year) but are not limited to them. They include the convenience of teachers (or other members) time schedule, the size and level of the pupil groups he (or she) teaches, the importance of his (or her) subject in the programme of the class, etc.

F1 Allocation of resources to the school.

F2 Use of resources within the school.
In **F1**, the point is to know who decides on, and how, the amount of school resources for teaching staff (**F1-1**), non-teaching staff (**F1-2**).
In **F2**, the point is to know who decides on, and how, the utilisation of these resources inside the school.
If a given level decides a global resource for staff, which an inferior level (the school, for example) divides between teaching and non-teaching staff, the right answer is that the inferior level decides for **F1-1** and **F1-2** in a framework decided by the superior level.
In the same way, if a superior level offers a grant, which an inferior level divides freely between teaching staff, non-teaching staff, capital expenditure or operating expenditures, the answer is that **F1-1, F1-2, F1-3** and **F1-4** are decided by the inferior level in a framework decided by the superior level.

Notes on the development of decision-making structures in education

These notes have been drafted by the participating countries as a framework for analysing quantitative material in the questionnaires, and are presented in their original language.

AUSTRIA

There is a long tradition of parent involvement in schools, via parent associations (*Elternvereine*), in Austria. These associations had no formal rights, but were still influential in schools. In the 1970s, formal scope for decision-making at ISCED 2 and 3 was introduced by the social democrat government.

The "*Klassenforen*" – democratic bodies at class level – and the "*Schulforen*" – democratic bodies at school level – offered greater scope for parent and pupil information. Decision-making was very restricted, and confined to the selection of school books and various matters to do with events at school. " *Elternbeirat*" (advisory board of parents) and *Bundesschülerbeirat* (advisory board of pupils) were established to advise the Minister for Education and the Arts; they had no decision-making powers. The *Bundesschülerbeirat* now has a statutory base and some formal rights, albeit very restricted. It is seen as training in political culture for pupils. The two strongest groups in the *Bundesschülerbeirat* are aligned with the two main political parties in the country.

An important change concerning school autonomy was enacted in July 1993. Within a clearly defined framework, the power to amend the curriculum at school level was transferred from the Ministry directly to individual schools. Such decisions require a two-thirds quorum of parents, teachers and pupils (the latter only at ISCED 2 and 3). A great deal of political discussion was involved.

The representatives of Austria's provinces argued for such powers to be delegated to the provinces; the Minister for Education and the Arts, backed by the social democrat party, preferred to transfer these powers directly to schools.

Last year, for schools coming directly under the Ministry of Education ("*Bundesschulen*") the ceiling for financial decision-making at school level was raised (from Sch. 5 000 to Sch. 50 000 per case).

Financial decision-making for public schools at ISCED 1 and 2 (except for the first cycle of higher-level schools) is a matter for their communities.

No further fundamental changes are expected in the near future. The number of decisions taken at school level will increase. Direct election of mayors and governors is under discussion and candidates' personalities accordingly become more important than their party political affiliations.

BELGIUM/BELGIQUE

La Belgique a connu dans son passé récent une révision fondamentale de sa Constitution. Les structures politiques, législatives et administratives de l'État belge se sont orientées vers un système fédéral, répartissant les pouvoirs entre l'État central, les communautés culturelles, les régions, les provinces et les communes. Cette nouvelle répartition n'a pas été sans incidences sur l'organisation de l'enseignement.

Toutefois, en Belgique, l'enseignement n'a jamais été organisé de façon homogène et centralisée. En effet, la première rédaction de la constitution (1830), s'appuyant sur le principe de la liberté de l'enseignement associée à une certaine autonomie reconnue aux communes et aux provinces, a permis le développement de réseaux d'enseignement plus ou moins autonomes. Nous brosserons un tableau synthétique – probablement caricatural – des structures de décision des trois principaux réseaux, à savoir l'enseignement de l'État, l'enseignement officiel subventionné, géré par les communes et les provinces, et enfin l'enseignement libre confessionnel (catholique) subventionné.

Si l'enseignement de l'État pouvait être qualifié de centralisé et l'enseignement officiel subventionné de mixte (les communes et les provinces jouant un rôle certain dans les décisions relatives à la gestion), l'enseignement libre était résolument décentralisé, laissant à l'établissement la quasi-totalité des décisions. Cet enseignement libre, ou plutôt ces établissements libres, bénéficiaient pourtant des mêmes subventions que les établissements officiels. Suivant le niveau d'études et la région concernée, ils rassemblaient environ cinquante pour cent de la population scolaire.

Les modifications apportées à la constitution, adoptées le 15 juillet 1988, ont placé les compétences en matière d'organisation de l'enseignement au niveau des trois communautés culturelles et linguistiques: flamande, francophone et germanophone.

Il convient dès lors d'envisager la structure actuelle des modes et des niveaux de décision engendrée par la répartition moins centralisée des pouvoirs, celle-ci ne simplifiant pas le paysage organisationnel de l'enseignement belge.

L'organisation de l'enseignement dans la Communauté flamande

Dès l'adoption de l'organisation de l'enseignement au niveau communautaire, un accord politique a permis la création d'un conseil autonome de l'enseignement au niveau de la communauté, réel pouvoir organisateur ayant pour rôle de gérer l'enseignement de la communauté (ex État) en lieu et place du Ministre. Cet organe se compose d'un conseil central mis en place en 1989, et de conseils locaux mis en place, progressivement, depuis septembre 1990. Les conseils locaux comportent une quinzaine de membres représentant partiellement les parents, les représentants des milieux sociaux, culturels et économiques, les représentants des enseignants et des directeurs d'établissements.

Cette volonté de promouvoir la participation accrue des parents, des personnels et de la société en général dans la gestion des établissements scolaires s'est traduite par un nouveau décret qui a pris effet en août 1991; il impose aux réseaux officiels et libres subventionnés de mettre en place des conseils locaux similaires. Leur implantation est en cours.

L'organisation de l'enseignement dans les Communautés francophone et germanophone

L'enseignement dans la communauté (ex État) a subi peu de modifications quant à ses structures de décision. Un conseil de l'éducation et de la formation a été mis en place. Sorte de conseil des sages, il tente de redéfinir les finalités de l'éducation en fonction des exigences nouvelles de la société et les moyens à mettre en œuvre pour les atteindre. Il réunit des responsables de réseau, des représentants syndicaux, des représentants des enseignants et des directeurs d'établissements, des experts, des représentants des milieux culturels, économiques et sociaux.

L'enseignement libre subventionné a adopté un statut spécifique pour le personnel relevant de son réseau. Ces nouvelles dispositions statutaires ont plusieurs effets sur les lieux et modes de décision. D'une part, elles comblent des lacunes en matière de protection des personnels, mais, d'autre part, elles restreignent fortement l'autonomie des établissements scolaires en officialisant la structure du réseau dont les instances centrales disposent d'un réel pouvoir de décision dans le domaine de la gestion du personnel.

Les perspectives

Que se soit au nord ou au sud du pays, il semble que les tendances de l'évolution des structures de décision suivent une même orientation. D'une part, nous assistons à une décentralisation accrue des lieux de décision, visant à terme à une plus grande autonomie des établissements ou de petites entités d'établissement, et d'autre part à une implication plus grande de tous les acteurs (enseignants, parents, élèves ou étudiants, représentants des milieux culturel, social et économique) non seulement dans le débat sur le devenir de l'enseignement mais aussi dans la gestion quotidienne des établissements scolaires.

FINLAND

The most important provisions pertaining to education are laid down in the constitution and educational legislation. The overall principles of educational policy are decided by the Parliament. The Government, the Ministry of Education and the National Board of Education are responsible for implementing these principles.

The Ministry of Education is headed by two ministers: the Minister of Education and the Minister of Culture. The Ministry of Education prepares educational bills. It also drafts decisions on education for the government and the Ministry itself. The National Board of Education is responsible for practical school administration, as well as educational planning and its implementation. For example, the Ministry of Education has the overall responsibility for planning major reforms, whereas the National Board of Education plans and develops national curricula and syllabi. In other words, the National Board is an expert office responsible for developing educational objectives, contents, methods and organisation.

Finland is divided into 12 administrative regions, *i.e.* provinces. These provinces are administered by regional governments, headed by a governor. Each provincial government also has a school department. Earlier, these departments mainly dealt with general education. Since 1987, however, when the Act on the National Board of Vocational Education and Regional Administration Subordinate to It came into force, the provincial governments have also handled matters pertaining to vocational training and acted as regional authorities. Before that, in the 1970s, they only dealt with some tasks relating to the reform of secondary education and training.

The Finnish regional administration has no representative bodies with decision-making power. The civil servants are assisted by advisory bodies comprised of appointed representatives. Such bodies were set up to assist the regional authorities to implement the extensive school reform launched in the seventies. For instance, a planning body was appointed in each province to effect the change from the old primary school system to the system of comprehensive schools. Similar planning bodies have been set up to prepare the implementation of reform of general and vocational secondary education in the provinces. They are consulted and make proposals for the development of secondary education. The provincial governments also have councils to take care of matters concerning student selection for general and vocational education.

On the local level, self-governing municipalities are responsible for the provision and administration of education. The main policy decisions are made by municipal councils. The municipal council appoints the municipal board, which prepares matters to be discussed by the council and implements the decisions taken by it. The council appoints various boards to carry out specific tasks. In terms of education, the most important of these is the school board.

The school board guides and supervises instruction in municipal schools and gives instructions for the arrangement of school work.

All comprehensive and upper secondary schools are run locally. They have a governing board, where teachers and other school staff as well as pupils' parents are represented. The governing board is in charge of tasks related to the development of school work and promotes co-operation between school and home.

The basic organizational structure explained above took shape in the 1970s with the minor exception that until the 1980s, there were no governing boards in the schools but instead school councils, which did not have any decision-making power of their own. In the 1970s, the school administration was highly centralized. The central government controlled schools even in details. The school's rules and regulations and the municipal curriculum were approved in the provincial government; it also set objectives for school work, conducted annual evaluations, and allocated resources in the form of grants. Teaching materials were approved by the central government. The school terms – *i.e.* beginning and ending dates and holidays – were also determined by the central government. Decisions on whether certain teaching groups should be established were made either by provincial government or by the National Board of General Education. Until the mid-1980s, appointments to educational posts had to be submitted for provincial government approval.

In 1985 decision-making power in these matters was delegated to local level, and decisions were taken by the school board of the municipality. The provincial office retained mainly some guidance and training functions. The National Board of General Education was responsible for designing the basic guidelines for curricula, among other things. The purpose of the guidelines was to help the planning of a curriculum at local level. In the 1990s, decentralization continued and decision-making power was further devolved to municipalities and to individual schools. Within central government, two separate national boards were merged (1992): the National Board of General Education and the National Board of Vocational Education became simply the National Board of Education. At provincial level, education duties have been reduced and are nowadays mainly related to vocational education. The municipalities are quite free to arrange their own administration of education as they think best. Since 1992 the law no longer specifically requires school boards or governing boards for schools. The only requirement is some kind of municipal body to take care of school matters.

More changes are going to take place in 1994, when the National Board of Education will no longer have any administrative tasks and will become the Finnish Educational Agency. How educational administration at provincial level will be organized in the future is still an open question. Similar trends as in the administration in general are also affecting vocational training. Future reforms will further enlarge the decision-making scope of local authorities and schools in matters relating to teaching arrangements and educational content.

Main functions of each of the decision-making levels in a nutshell

The government
- proposes bills and budget for the Parliament and statutes for the President;
- decides on the development plan for education (a framework regarding *e.g.* educational structure and scale for a limited period of time);
- decides on establishment and abolition of educational institutions, and on essential changes.

The Ministry of Education
- decides on appropriations and is in charge of grants to municipal and private vocational institutions;

– decides on the educational structure and on the provision of vocational education by provinces, by language groups and by sectors and levels of education.

The National Board of Education

– decides on the national basis for curricula, evaluates teaching and instruction and provides supporting services for the Ministry of Education and for the institutes;
– is in charge of keeping accounts for state schools.

Provincial governments

– decide on the range of vocational education;
– in charge of grants in certain cases.

The governing board of a school

– approves the school's rules and regulations and decides on the curriculum, appoints the headmaster and teachers and decides on the use of funds.

The government and the Ministry of Education are responsible for education policy, the National Board of Education for the development and evaluation of education, provincial governments for the range of education and the institutions together with their students for learning to learn and for the achievement of general and vocational skills and abilities.

FRANCE

L'évolution des processus de décision
dans l'enseignement depuis 1970

Le préambule de la Constitution de la République dispose que "l'organisation de l'enseignement public gratuit et laïque à tous les degrés est un devoir de l'État".

Dans ce cadre l'État a organisé depuis le début des années 1970 la dévolution de nombreuses prérogatives à des instances autres que l'administration centrale du ministère de l'Éducation: soit aux échelons locaux de l'administration d'État, dont la marge d'autonomie s'est accrue; soit à des collectivités territoriales élues; soit à l'établissement scolaire lui-même, qui a acquis, dans le second degré, le statut d'Établissement Public Local.

Cependant, la détermination des objectifs de la scolarisation et celle des programmes, la formation des maîtres, le contrôle de l'enseignement, la sanction des études, les conditions de recrutement, voire le recrutement des enseignants du second degré restent, pour l'essentiel, de la compétence de l'Administration centrale. Il en va de même de l'enseignement supérieur, à ceci près que les établissements d'enseignement supérieur disposent d'une forte autonomie pédagogique.

La déconcentration des décisions vers les échelons locaux de l'administration d'État

Depuis vingt ans, le ministère de l'Éducation nationale transfère progressivement une part importante de ses responsabilités de gestion à ses services régionaux (les rectorats d'académie) ou départementaux (les inspections académiques).

Il s'agit, en particulier, de la répartition des moyens d'enseignement entre les établissements scolaires, de l'organisation de certains examens, du recrutement des personnels non titulaires, de la gestion des personnels titulaires après leur recrutement, de l'organisation de la formation continue des enseignants et de la contribution des établissements d'enseignement à la formation continue.

La décentralisation

La décentralisation, c'est-à-dire le transfert de prérogatives de l'État à des collectivités territoriales élues par les citoyens (conseils régionaux, conseils généraux pour les départements, municipalités pour les communes), s'est appliquée aussi au système éducatif, en particulier dans le cadre de la loi du 22 juillet 1983.

D'une part, les départements et les régions ont bénéficié pour les collèges et les lycées des prérogatives dont les communes disposaient déjà pour les écoles primaires: financement des investissement et du fonctionnement matériel des établissements, et les départements sont devenus pleinement responsables des transports scolaires.

D'autre part, les collectivités territoriales ont reçu des compétences nouvelles, notamment en matière de planification de l'enseignement (prévoir les besoins d'enseignement et planifier la mise à disposition de formations adaptées). Elles ont aussi le droit d'organiser et de rémunérer des activités facultatives et complémentaires aux activités d'enseignement, d'utiliser les locaux scolaires hors des heures de classe. Les maires ont le pouvoir de décider des horaires scolaires dans l'enseignement primaire.

En outre, les collectivités territoriales sont maintenant représentées dans le conseil des écoles et des établissements du second degré.

Les établissements scolaires

Dans l'enseignement primaire, l'autonomie des écoles reste faible bien qu'elles puissent, depuis la "loi d'orientation" de 1989, proposer, dans le cadre de leur "projet d'école", certains aménagements de l'horaire des différentes matières, ou du cursus des élèves.

Les établissements du second degré disposent d'une plus grande autonomie. Dans le cadre de leur "projet d'établissement", ils peuvent en user dans les domaines de l'organisation de la pédagogie, de la vie des élèves dans l'établissement, de l'aide à l'insertion professionnelle, des relations avec l'environnement économique et social.

En particulier, on notera que si les programmes d'enseignement restent nationaux, les collèges (en 6e et 5e) et lycées (en seconde et première) disposent depuis 1990, de trois heures hebdomadaires, soit environ 10 pour cent de l'horaire, qu'ils peuvent utiliser avec une grande liberté.

Les élèves et leurs parents peuvent, dans une partie du territoire qui concerne environ la moitié des collèges et le tiers des lycées, demander à fréquenter un autre établissement que celui du secteur correspondant à leur domicile. Une commission départementale examine leur demande et y accède dans la grande majorité des cas.

Enfin, les établissements scolaires, qu'il s'agisse des écoles, des collèges ou des lycées, ont toujours bénéficié d'une très large autonomie – dont les modalités ont varié dans le temps – pour ce qui concerne les décisions individuelles relatives à la scolarité ou à l'orientation des élèves, sous réserve – bien sûr – de procédures d'appel ouvertes aux parents.

IRELAND

The principal change has been the introduction of boards of management, representative of school authorities, teachers and parents, for all ISCED level 1 schools and for a proportion of ISCED level 2 and level 3 schools. The boards of management were introduced for the different categories of schools in the 1970s, principally in 1972, 1974 and 1978. For all ISCED level schools and for voluntary secondary schools at ISCED level 2 and level 3 the establishment of boards of management has been a process of democratisation at school level and for vocational schools at ISCED level 2 and level 3 the process has been one of devolution from "Int" 1 to school level.

Schools, at all levels, have been given greater freedom to adapt curricular programmes to their individual needs.

There have not been any statutory changes in the status of administrative and elected bodies since 1970.

A Green Paper, *Education for a Changing World*, was published in 1992. Ongoing debate is taking place on its contents. The Minister for Education has announced that it is the intention of the Government to establish democratic structures at local level to carry out certain functions in educational administration. The precise functions of these structures will be set out in a White Paper and in legislation.

The Ministry of Education has a tradition of consulting regularly with Church authorities, local education authorities, organisations representing management bodies and teachers' unions about all educational matters. In recent years, greater formal recognition has been given to the role of parents in education. It is expected that parents' organisations will have an even greater role in education in the future.

PORTUGAL

In the last two decades major changes have been introduced in the structures of education administration and in the decision-making processes. A number of aspects can be singled out:

1.   Schools principals: the earlier appointment system was replaced by a school-based electoral process, giving teachers greater involvement and responsibility in school governance. This model was a consequence of the country's return to democracy, and was clearly intended to introduce a political approach to school administration, which carried with it a degree of ambiguity and dysfunctionality. Reforms are now being introduced to scale down the teachers' role in school structures and to give more scope to parents and local communities.

2.   The deconcentration of services: regional education services were established in order to devolve powers and duties away from the central administration; similar steps were taken right across government. They have little decision-making authority, and they tend to pattern themselves on the central services. Local school support centres have been set up within regional services, to bring the administration closer to the grassroots. All three levels of decision-making are increasingly enclosed in a statutory framework, and full autonomy and decisions by consensus are less common.

3.   The inspectorate: to achieve fuller monitoring of school units, the inspection services gained importance during the 1980s. There is now more emphasis on the responsibility of schools and central services for effective education, rather than the political approach to administration.

4.   The education reform: the reforms also introduced changes throughout education administration, reducing the importance of the central services in particular as regards their earlier autonomous powers of decision. Decisions are now predominantly taken within a statutory framework, and schools have more say.

Compared with the regional and central services (level 2 or 3), schools have by and large been given greater responsibility (from 39 to 48 per cent). This does not mean greater autonomy, but a broader decision-making capability within the statutory framework (up from 27 per cent in 1991 to 41 per cent in 1993); all levels of administrative action are increasingly enclosed in that framework.

Regional services (level 2) have received broader powers of intervention and greater administrative responsibility. Their decision-making powers, however, have decreased proportionately. School responsibility for "planning-structures" has risen from 37 to 50 per cent, and for the "financial field" from 0 to 31 per cent.

These changes were part of a broader educational reform and current pressures seem to go in the direction of greater autonomy for schools and fuller monitoring and self-monitoring to bolster decision-making processes.

128

SPAIN/ESPAGNE

Évolution récente des structures de décision

En Espagne, les structures de décision dans l'enseignement présentent les caractéristiques suivantes:

1. L'existence de deux réseaux distincts: l'enseignement public et l'enseignement privé. Dans ce dernier, il faut distinguer le privé sous contrat, financé à 100 pour cent par l'État et le privé indépendant qui ne bénéficie d'aucun financement public.
2. La répartition du pouvoir entre l'administration centrale et 17 communautés autonomes, établie par la constitution de 1978. Un processus de décentralisation est en cours, à la fin duquel la gestion d'ensemble de l'enseignement sera dans sa plus grande partie de la compétence des communautés autonomes.
3. En 1990-91, date de référence de l'étude sur les processus de décision, le transfert des compétences en matière d'enseignement avait été notifié à seulement sept communautés autonomes, concernant environ 60 pour cent des élèves. Dans le territoire des dix autres communautés autonomes, l'enseignement est encore géré par le ministère de l'Éducation. Cette dualité dans la structure de décision se reflète dans les données pour l'Espagne concernant les niveaux intermédiaire, supérieur et national.
4. Au niveau local, les communes n'ont presque pas de compétences en matière d'enseignement. Dans cette étude, le niveau intermédiaire inférieur fait référence aux pouvoirs publics qui gèrent les matières enseignées dans les provinces.

En 1984, il a été décidé d'établir dans toutes les écoles publiques ou privées sous contrat un conseil scolaire qui exerce la plus grande autorité dans l'établissement. Le conseil scolaire est constitué de représentants des communes, des professeurs, des élèves, des parents et du personnel non-enseignant. Les directeurs d'établissement sont élus par ce conseil qui a aussi d'autres attributions: il approuve le plan annuel d'activité, le projet pédagogique, le règlement intérieur de discipline, les activités en dehors de l'école, le budget annuel et l'état des comptes.

Il faut aussi indiquer que, dans le système d'enseignement espagnol, l'évaluation des connaissances se fait normalement par contrôle continu. En général, il n'existe pas d'examens externes ni d'examens spécifiques requis pour l'obtention d'un diplôme. La délivrance d'un diplôme est proposée par les professeurs d'après le rendement de l'élève au cours de l'année scolaire. La seule exception se situe à la fin du cycle secondaire: les élèves doivent passer un examen spécifique pour avoir accès à l'université.

Tendances futures

Dans les prochaines années, le processus de transfert des compétences en matière d'enseignement aux communautés autonomes sera achevé. Les seules compétences du ministère de l'Éducation seront alors la supervision générale du système, la fixation d'objectifs minimums pour l'enseignement, et l'homologation des diplômes.

Une réforme est actuellement en cours: elle prévoit que les établissements auront plus d'autonomie pour fixer les matières qui y seront enseignées ainsi que leur contenu spécifique. L'autonomie financière et l'autonomie en matière d'organisation, en particulier pour l'embauche du personnel enseignant et non-enseignant.

Deux notes d'interprétation

a) L'organisation scolaire existante en 1990-91 ne permet pas de distinguer les données relatives aux niveaux CITE 1 et 2. Les chiffres concernant ces deux niveaux sont donc les mêmes dans les tableaux.

b) En 1990-91, environ deux tiers des élèves des niveaux CITE 1, 2 et 3 sont accueillis dans les établissements publics et un tiers dans les établissements privés. Dans ce dernier tiers, 90 pour cent environ des élèves sont scolarisés dans des établissements privés sous contrat aux niveaux CITE 1 et 2, et 40 pour cent au niveau CITE 3. Étant donné que les établissements privés sans contrat ont plus d'autonomie de décision, cela explique les disparités qui apparaissent dans les tableaux entre les niveaux CITE dans l'enseignement privé.

SWEDEN

The National Agency for Education
Sweden's National School Administration

The Swedish school system rests on the principle of guaranteeing all children equivalent basic education, irrespective of residential locality or parental income for example. This is why goals and guidelines are determined by the *Riksdag* (Parliament) and why there is a national school administration.

National control of the school sector has been fundamentally transformed in recent years and greater responsibilities vested in the municipalities.

In the autumn of 1989, as part of the ongoing decentralisation of responsibilities and decision-making in the school sector, the *Riksdag* made municipalities responsible for teachers and other staff categories in the school sector.

As a result, the municipalities now have complete and undivided responsibility for school activities.

This policy decision also entailed the abolition, with effect from 30th June 1991, of the National Board of Education and the County Education Committees, and their replacement by two new and far smaller central authorities, of which the National Agency for Education is one.

Who decides what?

The Riksdag and government lay down general goals and guidelines for schools, mainly through the Education Act and the curricula.

The National Agency for Education is responsible for national follow-up and evaluation in the school sector. It also has the task of compiling input documentation and proposals for educational development, as well as contributing in other ways towards the development of the school sector.

Local education authorities are responsible for the conduct of school activities in accordance with the frames and guidelines established by the *Riksdag* and government.

The National Agency for Education is the central authority responsible for compulsory schools, upper secondary schools and (below post-secondary level) for adult education for formal competence.

The first of these main tasks requires the National Agency to develop and take responsibility for the follow-up and evaluation of public sector schooling. This applies both to the results of school activities and to their organisation and economics. To the tasks of follow-up and evaluation are added that of supervising the Swedish school system, above all by ensuring that the municipalities comply with the provisions of the Education Act and that the rights of the individual are respected.

The second main task of the National Agency is to develop the public sector school system. This involves compiling input documentation and proposals for educational development, which can mean development in a general sense and in the long term, but also modifications to national policy levels in limited fields or measures of a more short-term nature.

In addition, research in the school sector is to be encouraged.

The National Agency can be commissioned by the government to draw up syllabi or other policy instruments for the school sector.

The National Agency is required to submit annual achievement reports to the government, as well as extra detailed budget requests at three-yearly intervals.

The National Agency is to participate in the introduction and encouragement of change and development in schools. Evaluation results together with research findings, labour market developments and social developments generally will provide the basis for the changes recommended by the National Agency.

Information, curricula commentaries and in-service training are among the instruments to be used in developing the school system.

The National Agency is headquartered in Stockholm and also has a field organisation. At central level it comprises three divisions, an agency staff and a field staff.

The Basic Information Division is in charge of the follow-up systems and databases which activities require and supervises the implementation of criteria and models for national funding.

The Evaluation Division is responsible for national evaluation of schools in the light of information from databases and follow-up systems and also using documentation from the field organisations.

The Development Division takes part in educational development by drafting changes, assists in the implementation of changes and, at the instance of the government, draws up syllabi.

The Field Organisation is divided into eight regions, each with a Regional Director and a number of Directors of Education. The regions are divided into working areas, each of which corresponds to one or more municipalities. Each working area has a Director of Education whose duties include taking part in evaluation and development work in schools, supporting the municipalities and supervising schools. The field organisation reports directly to the Directorate and is co-ordinated at central level by the National Agency's *field staff.*

SWITZERLAND/SUISSE

Évolution des processus de décision depuis 1970

Les restrictions budgétaires (que connaissent la plupart des pays de l'OCDE) ont des conséquences sur le système éducatif. En Suisse, elles affectent en premier lieu les dépenses liées à la rémunération et à l'engagement du personnel éducatif (au sens large du terme: enseignants, encadrement, administration, recherche, etc.). Nous ne décelons pas pour autant de modifications sensibles en ce qui concerne les processus de décision.

En ce qui concerne les réformes (période 1970-1990), elles ont surtout porté sur l'organisation du système d'enseignement (durée de l'enseignement dans les différents niveaux et dans les écoles, perméabilité des filières, etc.), mais elles n'ont pas affecté les processus de décision en tant que tels.

Ce n'est un secret pour personne que la Suisse (en tant qu'État) est un pays fédéraliste. Dans le domaine de l'éducation, ce mode de fonctionnement est particulièrement développé. Son origine remonte à plusieurs siècles.

Ce fonctionnement très décentralisé, auquel s'ajoute la grande stabilité des institutions, n'a pas connu de modifications notables au cours des dernières décennies. Cela est valable pour les niveaux CITE 1, 2 et 3.

De ce fait, nous n'observons pas de changements significatifs dans les processus de décision: c'est ainsi qu'il n'y a pas eu de transferts de compétence vers le "bas". En gardant à l'esprit les dimensions réduites du pays, il est difficile, voire impossible, de décentraliser davantage.

Une question subsiste: comparés à ceux d'autres pays, les établissements ont peu, ou moins, de compétences en matière de décision. Cela peut s'expliquer par la proximité des centres de décision. Les écoles y participent d'une manière ou d'une autre. Nous ne connaissons pas d'indices qui pourraient nous conduire à penser que la situation changera dans les années à venir.

A l'inverse, une certaine réorientation des prises de décision vers le "haut" pourrait éventuellement se produire. La nécessaire compatibilité des diplômes entre cantons et par rapport à l'Europe pourrait entraîner une augmentation du pouvoir de décision des instances de la Confédération. Cela concerne en premier lieu le secondaire supérieur (CITE 3).

UNITED STATES

There have been a number of developments in the structure of decision-making in the United States since 1970. However, these developments do not reflect official changes in the structure of the national education system but rather changes in the use of the existing decision-making authority. Key developments are discussed below:

National level. Much of the national government's involvement in education decision-making stems from its role in ensuring equal opportunity, civil rights and general national well-being.

Increases in national involvement in decision-making during the 1970s and 1980s occurred in response to the civil rights movement and the United States reaction to Sputnik. The 1965 Elementary and Secondary Education Act (ESEA), the Education for all Handicapped Children Act of 1975, and the Bilingual Education Act of 1968 are examples of federal legislation that establish a framework for state level decision-making. These legislative acts made national funding available for certain education programmes, providing states and local education systems met specified conditions. The national courts have also made decisions that effect education, including decisions that defined the role of religion in the schools and guaranteed academic freedom to teachers and students.

State level. State involvement in decision-making is primarily through setting a framework for intermediate and school-level decision-making. State activity in the area of education decision-making has become more noticeable since 1970 as states asserted their authority in new and different ways. For instance, many states have introduced minimum competency examinations and new course requirements for graduation since 1970. Additionally, a number of state courts have made decisions in the area of finance that have affected the way state and local jurisdictions can raise funds for education. The states have also influenced decision-making indirectly through their focus on standards and accountability. Since 1970, many states have started requiring districts to provide regular information about how their schools are performing in an effort to stimulate accountability. These annual "reports cards" typically contain information about student demographics and academic performance, teacher qualifications and demographics, instructional processes and quality, and financial information. The push by the states toward increased accountability at the district level was followed, in the mid-1980s, by the call for national standards and tests set forth by the nation's governors.

Below the state level. Since 1970, there has been a move to decentralize education decision making to the school level (in some decision areas). This trend intensified in the late 1980s and continues at an accelerated pace today. However, it is important to note that, while some schools have adopted school-based management, others have not. Further, the extent to which schools make decisions, as well as the nature of school-based management activities, varies considerably across schools.

Schools have become increasingly active in decisions concerning education processes. However, they do not typically have the authority to set the criteria for measuring education outcomes used for accountability or graduation by the states.

In places where there is increased decision-making activity by states and a trend towards school-based decision-making, the role of districts in education decision-making may be affected.

Future trends

Several future trends in the structure of education decision-making are anticipated. On the one hand, while participants at all levels are taking part in the development of national standards, once adopted, these standards will provide a unified national framework within which other levels can make decisions. At the same time, the trend toward site- or school-based management of education continues.

List of national correspondents, responsible for the survey in their respective countries

Dr. Helmut BACHMANN
Zentrum für Schulversuch
und Schulentwicklung
Klagenfurt
AUSTRIA

Ms. Marleen BRONDERS
Vrije Universiteit Brussel
Brussels
BELGIUM

Mr. Poul LASSEN
Ministry of Education
Copenhagen
DENMARK

Mr. Erkki KANGASNIEMI
University of Jyvaskyla
Jyvaskyla
FINLAND

Mr. Denis MEURET
Ministère de l'Éducation Nationale
Paris
FRANCE

Mr. Reinhard SCHANZ
Ministerialrat
Niedersächsisches Kultusministerium
Hannover
GERMANY

Mr. Sean HUNT
Department of Education
Dublin
IRELAND

Mr. James IRVING
Ministry of Education
Wellington
NEW ZEALAND

Mrs Bodhild BAASLAND
Ministry of Education, Research
and Church Affairs
Oslo
NORWAY

Ms. Carmo CLIMACO
Ministério de Educação
Lisbon
PORTUGAL

Mr. Ramon PAJARES-BOX
Técnica de Educación
Madrid
SPAIN

Ms. Brigitta ANDREN
Skolverket
Stockholm
SWEDEN

Mrs Lisbeth RUDEMO
National Board of Education
Stockholm
SWEDEN

Mr. Jacques PROD'HOM
Office fédéral de la Statistique
Bern
SWITZERLAND

Mr. Eugen STOCKER
Office fédéral de la Statistique
Bern
SWITZERLAND

Mrs Laura SALGANIK
Pelavin Associates
Washington, D.C.
UNITED STATES

ALSO AVAILABLE

Education at a Glance - OECD Indicators
FF 220   FFE 285   £35   US$ 54   DM 83

OECD Education Statistics, 1985-1992/Statistiques de l'enseignement de l'OCDE, 1985-1992 (bilingual)
FF 160   FFE 210   £25   US$ 40   DM 60

Measuring the Quality of Schools/Mesurer la qualité des établissements scolaires (bilingual)
FF 120   FFE 155   £20   US$ 29   DM 47

Measuring What Students Learn/Mesurer les résultats scolaires (bilingual)
FF 110   FFE 140   £17   US$ 27   DM 40

Education and Employment/Formation et emploi (bilingual)
FF 90   FFE 115   £14   US$ 22   DM 34

Public Expectations of the Final Stage of Compulsory Education/Le dernier cycle de l'enseignement obligatoire : quelle attente ? (bilingual)
FF 100   FFE 130   £16   US$ 25   DM 38

Prices charged at the OECD Bookshop.
The OECD CATALOGUE OF PUBLICATIONS and supplements will be sent free of charge
on request addressed either to OECD Publications Service,
or to the OECD Distributor in your country.

MAIN SALES OUTLETS OF OECD PUBLICATIONS
PRINCIPAUX POINTS DE VENTE DES PUBLICATIONS DE L'OCDE

ARGENTINA – ARGENTINE
Carlos Hirsch S.R.L.
Galería Güemes, Florida 165, 4° Piso
1333 Buenos Aires   Tel. (1) 331.1787 y 331.2391
                                Telefax: (1) 331.1787

AUSTRALIA – AUSTRALIE
D.A. Information Services
648 Whitehorse Road, P.O.B 163
Mitcham, Victoria 3132   Tel. (03) 873.4411
                                    Telefax: (03) 873.5679

AUSTRIA – AUTRICHE
Gerold & Co.
Graben 31
Wien I   Tel. (0222) 533.50.14
                    Telefax: (0222) 512.47.31.29

BELGIUM – BELGIQUE
Jean De Lannoy
Avenue du Roi 202 Koningslaan
B-1060 Bruxelles   Tel. (02) 538.51.69/538.08.41
                            Telefax: (02) 538.08.41

CANADA
Renouf Publishing Company Ltd.
1294 Algoma Road
Ottawa, ON K1B 3W8   Tel. (613) 741.4333
                                Telefax: (613) 741.5439
Stores:
61 Sparks Street
Ottawa, ON K1P 5R1   Tel. (613) 238.8985
211 Yonge Street
Toronto, ON M5B 1M4   Tel. (416) 363.3171
                                Telefax: (416)363.59.63

Les Éditions La Liberté Inc.
3020 Chemin Sainte-Foy
Sainte-Foy, PQ G1X 3V6   Tel. (418) 658.3763
                                Telefax: (418) 658.3763

Federal Publications Inc.
165 University Avenue, Suite 701
Toronto, ON M5H 3B8   Tel. (416) 860.1611
                                Telefax: (416) 860.1608

Les Publications Fédérales
1185 Université
Montréal, QC H3B 3A7   Tel. (514) 954.1633
                                Telefax: (514) 954.1635

CHINA – CHINE
China National Publications Import
Export Corporation (CNPIEC)
16 Gongti E. Road, Chaoyang District
P.O. Box 88 or 50
Beijing 100704 PR   Tel. (01) 506.6688
                            Telefax: (01) 506.3101

CHINESE TAIPEI – TAIPEI CHINOIS
Good Faith Worldwide Int'l. Co. Ltd.
9th Floor, No. 118, Sec. 2
Chung Hsiao E. Road
Taipei   Tel. (02) 391.7396/391.7397
                        Telefax: (02) 394.9176

CZECH REPUBLIC – RÉPUBLIQUE TCHÈQUE
Artia Pegas Press Ltd.
Narodni Trida 25
POB 825
111 21 Praha 1   Tel. 26.65.68
                        Telefax: 26.20.81

DENMARK – DANEMARK
Munksgaard Book and Subscription Service
35, Nørre Søgade, P.O. Box 2148
DK-1016 København K   Tel. (33) 12.85.70
                                Telefax: (33) 12.93.87

EGYPT – ÉGYPTE
Middle East Observer
41 Sherif Street
Cairo   Tel. 392.6919
                        Telefax: 360-6804

FINLAND – FINLANDE
Akateeminen Kirjakauppa
Keskuskatu 1, P.O. Box 128
00100 Helsinki
Subscription Services/Agence d'abonnements :
P.O. Box 23
00371 Helsinki   Tel. (358 0) 121 4416
                            Telefax: (358 0) 121.4450

FRANCE
OECD/OCDE
Mail Orders/Commandes par correspondance:
2, rue André-Pascal
75775 Paris Cedex 16   Tel. (33-1) 45.24.82.00
                            Telefax: (33-1) 49.10.42.76
                                    Telex: 640048 OCDE
Internet: Compte.PUBSINQ @ oecd.org
Orders via Minitel, France only/
Commandes par Minitel, France exclusivement :
36 15 OCDE
OECD Bookshop/Librairie de l'OCDE :
33, rue Octave-Feuillet
75016 Paris   Tel. (33-1) 45.24.81.81
                            (33-1) 45.24.81.67
Documentation Française
29, quai Voltaire
75007 Paris   Tel. 40.15.70.00
Gibert Jeune (Droit-Économie)
6, place Saint-Michel
75006 Paris   Tel. 43.25.91.19
Librairie du Commerce International
10, avenue d'Iéna
75016 Paris   Tel. 40.73.34.60
Librairie Dunod
Université Paris-Dauphine
Place du Maréchal de Lattre de Tassigny
75016 Paris   Tel. (1) 44.05.40.13
Librairie Lavoisier
11, rue Lavoisier
75008 Paris   Tel. 42.65.39.95
Librairie L.G.D.J. - Montchrestien
20, rue Soufflot
75005 Paris   Tel. 46.33.89.85
Librairie des Sciences Politiques
30, rue Saint-Guillaume
75007 Paris   Tel. 45.48.36.02
P.U.F.
49, boulevard Saint-Michel
75005 Paris   Tel. 43.25.83.40
Librairie de l'Université
12a, rue Nazareth
13100 Aix-en-Provence   Tel. (16) 42.26.18.08
Documentation Française
165, rue Garibaldi
69003 Lyon   Tel. (16) 78.63.32.23
Librairie Decitre
29, place Bellecour
69002 Lyon   Tel. (16) 72.40.54.54
Librairie Sauramps
Le Triangle
34967 Montpellier Cedex 2   Tel. (16) 67.58.85.15
                            Tekefax: (16) 67.58.27.36

GERMANY – ALLEMAGNE
OECD Publications and Information Centre
August-Bebel-Allee 6
D-53175 Bonn   Tel. (0228) 959.120
                            Telefax: (0228) 959.12.17

GREECE – GRÈCE
Librairie Kauffmann
Mavrokordatou 9
106 78 Athens   Tel. (01) 32.55.321
                            Telefax: (01) 32.30.320

HONG-KONG
Swindon Book Co. Ltd.
Astoria Bldg. 3F
34 Ashley Road, Tsimshatsui
Kowloon, Hong Kong   Tel. 2376.2062
                            Telefax: 2376.0685

HUNGARY – HONGRIE
Euro Info Service
Margitsziget, Európa Ház
1138 Budapest   Tel. (1) 111.62.16
                            Telefax: (1) 111.60.61

ICELAND – ISLANDE
Mál Mog Menning
Laugavegi 18, Pósthólf 392
121 Reykjavik   Tel. (1) 552.4240
                            Telefax: (1) 562.3523

INDIA – INDE
Oxford Book and Stationery Co.
Scindia House
New Delhi 110001   Tel. (11) 331.5896/5308
                            Telefax: (11) 332.5993
17 Park Street
Calcutta 700016   Tel. 240832

INDONESIA – INDONÉSIE
Pdii-Lipi
P.O. Box 4298
Jakarta 12042   Tel. (21) 573.34.67
                            Telefax: (21) 573.34.67

IRELAND – IRLANDE
Government Supplies Agency
Publications Section
4/5 Harcourt Road
Dublin 2   Tel. 661.31.11
                            Telefax: 475.27.60

ISRAEL
Praedicta
5 Shatner Street
P.O. Box 34030
Jerusalem 91430   Tel. (2) 52.84.90/1/2
                            Telefax: (2) 52.84.93
R.O.Y. International
P.O. Box 13056
Tel Aviv 61130   Tel. (3) 546 1423
                            Telefax: (3) 546 1442
Palestinian Authority/Middle East:
INDEX Information Services
P.O.B. 19502
Jerusalem   Tel. (2) 27.12.19
                            Telefax: (2) 27.16.34

ITALY – ITALIE
Libreria Commissionaria Sansoni
Via Duca di Calabria 1/1
50125 Firenze   Tel. (055) 64.54.15
                            Telefax: (055) 64.12.57
Via Bartolini 29
20155 Milano   Tel. (02) 36.50.83
Editrice e Libreria Herder
Piazza Montecitorio 120
00186 Roma   Tel. 679.46.28
                            Telefax: 678.47.51
Libreria Hoepli
Via Hoepli 5
20121 Milano   Tel. (02) 86.54.46
                            Telefax: (02) 805.28.86
Libreria Scientifica
Dott. Lucio de Biasio 'Aeiou'
Via Coronelli, 6
20146 Milano   Tel. (02) 48.95.45.52
                            Telefax: (02) 48.95.45.48

JAPAN – JAPON
OECD Publications and Information Centre
Landic Akasaka Building
2-3-4 Akasaka, Minato-ku
Tokyo 107   Tel. (81.3) 3586.2016
                            Telefax: (81.3) 3584.7929

KOREA – CORÉE
Kyobo Book Centre Co. Ltd.
P.O. Box 1658, Kwang Hwa Moon
Seoul   Tel. 730.78.91
                            Telefax: 735.00.30

MALAYSIA – MALAISIE
University of Malaya Bookshop
University of Malaya
P.O. Box 1127, Jalan Pantai Baru
59700 Kuala Lumpur
Malaysia   Tel. 756.5000/756.5425
                            Telefax: 756.3246

MEXICO – MEXIQUE
Revistas y Periodicos Internacionales S.A. de C.V.
Florencia 57 - 1004
Mexico, D.F. 06600   Tel. 207.81.00
                             Telefax: 208.39.79

NETHERLANDS – PAYS-BAS
SDU Uitgeverij Plantijnstraat
Externe Fondsen
Postbus 20014
2500 EA's-Gravenhage   Tel. (070) 37.89.880
Voor bestellingen: Telefax: (070) 34.75.778

NEW ZEALAND
NOUVELLE-ZÉLANDE
GPLegislation Services
P.O. Box 12418
Thorndon, Wellington   Tel. (04) 496.5655
                            Telefax: (04) 496.5698

NORWAY – NORVÈGE
Narvesen Info Center – NIC
Bertrand Narvesens vei 2
P.O. Box 6125 Etterstad
0602 Oslo 6   Tel. (022) 57.33.00
                            Telefax: (022) 68.19.01

PAKISTAN
Mirza Book Agency
65 Shahrah Quaid-E-Azam
Lahore 54000   Tel. (42) 353.601
                            Telefax: (42) 231.730

PHILIPPINE – PHILIPPINES
International Book Center
5th Floor, Filipinas Life Bldg.
Ayala Avenue
Metro Manila   Tel. 81.96.76
                            Telex 23312 RHP PH

PORTUGAL
Livraria Portugal
Rua do Carmo 70-74
Apart. 2681
1200 Lisboa   Tel. (01) 347.49.82/5
                            Telefax: (01) 347.02.64

SINGAPORE – SINGAPOUR
Gower Asia Pacific Pte Ltd.
Golden Wheel Building
41, Kallang Pudding Road, No. 04-03
Singapore 1334   Tel. 741.5166
                            Telefax: 742.9356

SPAIN – ESPAGNE
Mundi-Prensa Libros S.A.
Castelló 37, Apartado 1223
Madrid 28001   Tel. (91) 431.33.99
                            Telefax: (91) 575.39.98

Libreria Internacional AEDOS
Consejo de Ciento 391
08009 – Barcelona   Tel. (93) 488.30.09
                             Telefax: (93) 487.76.59

Llibreria de la Generalitat
Palau Moja
Rambla dels Estudis, 118
08002 – Barcelona
            (Subscripcions) Tel. (93) 318.80.12
            (Publicacions) Tel. (93) 302.67.23
                            Telefax: (93) 412.18.54

SRI LANKA
Centre for Policy Research
c/o Colombo Agencies Ltd.
No. 300-304, Galle Road
Colombo 3   Tel. (1) 574240, 573551-2
                        Telefax: (1) 575394, 510711

SWEDEN – SUÈDE
Fritzes Customer Service
S–106 47 Stockholm   Tel. (08) 690.90.90
                            Telefax: (08) 20.50.21

Subscription Agency/Agence d'abonnements :
Wennergren-Williams Info AB
P.O. Box 1305
171 25 Solna   Tel. (08) 705.97.50
                            Telefax: (08) 27.00.71

SWITZERLAND – SUISSE
Maditec S.A. (Books and Periodicals - Livres
et périodiques)
Chemin des Palettes 4
Case postale 266
1020 Renens VD 1   Tel. (021) 635.08.65
                           Telefax: (021) 635.07.80

Librairie Payot S.A.
4, place Pépinet
CP 3212
1002 Lausanne   Tel. (021) 341.33.47
                            Telefax: (021) 341.33.45

Librairie Unilivres
6, rue de Candolle
1205 Genève   Tel. (022) 320.26.23
                            Telefax: (022) 329.73.18

Subscription Agency/Agence d'abonnements :
Dynapresse Marketing S.A.
38 avenue Vibert
1227 Carouge   Tel. (022) 308.07.89
                            Telefax: (022) 308.07.99

See also – Voir aussi :
OECD Publications and Information Centre
August-Bebel-Allee 6
D-53175 Bonn (Germany)   Tel. (0228) 959.120
                           Telefax: (0228) 959.12.17

THAILAND – THAÏLANDE
Suksit Siam Co. Ltd.
113, 115 Fuang Nakhon Rd.
Opp. Wat Rajbopith
Bangkok 10200   Tel. (662) 225.9531/2
                            Telefax: (662) 222.5188

TURKEY – TURQUIE
Kültür Yayinlari Is-Türk Ltd. Sti.
Atatürk Bulvari No. 191/Kat 13
Kavaklidere/Ankara   Tel. 428.11.40 Ext. 2458
Dolmabahce Cad. No. 29
Besiktas/Istanbul   Tel. (312) 260 7188
                            Telex: (312) 418 29 46

UNITED KINGDOM – ROYAUME-UNI
HMSO
Gen. enquiries   Tel. (171) 873 8496
Postal orders only:
P.O. Box 276, London SW8 5DT
Personal Callers HMSO Bookshop
49 High Holborn, London WC1V 6HB
                            Telefax: (171) 873 8416
Branches at: Belfast, Birmingham, Bristol,
Edinburgh, Manchester

UNITED STATES – ÉTATS-UNIS
OECD Publications and Information Center
2001 L Street N.W., Suite 650
Washington, D.C. 20036-4910 Tel. (202) 785.6323
                            Telefax: (202) 785.0350

VENEZUELA
Libreria del Este
Avda F. Miranda 52, Aptdo. 60337
Edificio Galipán
Caracas 106   Tel. 951.1705/951.2307/951.1297
                        Telegram: Libreste Caracas

Subscription to OECD periodicals may also be
placed through main subscription agencies.

Les abonnements aux publications périodiques de
l'OCDE peuvent être souscrits auprès des
principales agences d'abonnement.

Orders and inquiries from countries where Distribu-
tors have not yet been appointed should be sent to:
OECD Publications Service, 2 rue André-Pascal,
75775 Paris Cedex 16, France.

Les commandes provenant de pays où l'OCDE n'a
pas encore désigné de distributeur peuvent être
adressées à : OCDE, Service des Publications,
2, rue André-Pascal, 75775 Paris Cedex 16, France.

7-1995

OECD PUBLICATIONS, 2 rue André-Pascal, 75775 PARIS CEDEX 16
PRINTED IN FRANCE
(96 95 03 1) ISBN 92-64-14421-8 - No. 47907 1995